Got problems?
Facing adversity?
Seeking direction?
Not sure what to do?
No idea where to turn?

It Is P.R.O.O.F. T.I.M.E.
There Is Hope!

André K Mickel

Copyright © 2015 by Andre' K Mickel

It's PROOF TIME...
There is Hope!
by Andre' K Mickel

Printed in the United States of America

Edited by Xulon Press

ISBN 9781498426275

All rights reserved solely by the author. The author guarantees all contents are original and do not infringe upon the legal rights of any other person or work. No part of this book may be reproduced in any form without the permission of the author. The views expressed in this book are not necessarily those of the publisher.

All quotes, unless otherwise noted, are from the New King James Version. Copyright 1979, 1980, 1982 by Thomas Nelson, Inc. Used by permission. All rights reserved.

Scriptures marked KJV are taken from The Holy Bible, King James Version. Copyright © 1972 by Thomas Nelson Inc., Camden, New Jersey 08103.

Scriptures marked NASB are taken from the NEW AMERICAN STANDARD BIBLE®, Copyright © 1960, 1962, 1963, 1971, 1972, 1973, 1975, 1977, 1995 by The Lockman Foundation, LaHabra, CA Used by permission. All rights reserved.

The Amplified Bible, containing the amplified Old Testament and the amplified New Testament. 1987. The Lockman Foundation: La Habra, CA

Published by permission. Originally published by NavPress in English as THE MESSAGE: The Bible in Contemporary Language copyright 2002 by Eugene Peterson. All rights reserved. (The Message Bible Online)

Scriptures marked NRSV are taken from the New Revised Standard Version Bible, copyright © 1989 the Division of Christian Education of the National Council of the Churches of Christ in the United States of America. Used by permission. All rights reserved.

Scriptures marked NLT are from the New Living Translation copyright© 1996, 2004, 2007 by Tyndale House Foundation. Used by permission of Tyndale House Publishers Inc., Carol Stream, Illinois 60188. All rights reserved.

Scriptures marked NET are from the New English Translation of the Bible® copyright ©1996-2006 by Biblical Studies Press, L.L.C. http://netbible.com All rights reserved.

Scriptures marked ERV are from the Easy-to-Read Version of the Bible copyright © 2006 by World Bible Translation Center.

www.xulonpress.com

Dedication

I dedicate this book to the One who taught me to tie my shoes. To the One who has prayed over me and for me all of my life... and who taught me to pray. To the One who is my example of what it means to model Christ Jesus and sacrifice herself for so many including me. To the One who introduced me to my Lord and Savior Jesus Christ. To the One who taught me the meaning of hard work and getting a good education. To my best friend: I love you Mom, Lovie Ann Mickel.

To my Father, Archy Delano Mickel, who taught me: "If you are going to do something, do it right!" I am still working on it dad, and I have a long way to go! Put in a good word for me up in heaven!

To my two older brothers Reverend Julius Mickel and Coach Steven Mickel: Thank you for the years of care, big brotherly guidance and love. I could have never made it this far without the time you two invested in me.

To the "Love of my life," my wife, Mrs. Estomarys Mickel!!

To Pastor Bennie Mosely, Angie Mosely, and the entire Mosely family of the Christian Teaching Center Church in Akron, Ohio... YOU are the strongest man and family I know! Thank you for all of your prayers, concern, and each and every PERSONAL Wednesday and Thursday Afternoon session breaking the bread of the Word with my family.

TABLE OF CONTENTS

Preface: You Are Not Alone! vii

Introduction: Yes, I Will Help You xiii

Chapter 1:   Where Is Your Proof? 19

Chapter 2:   It Is P.R.O.O.F. T.I.M.E. 28

Chapter 3:   "P" Is for Praise 46

Chapter 4:   "R' Is for Remember 62

Chapter 5:   "O" Is for Obedience – The Solution
                 to Every Problem 79

Chapter 6:   "O" Is for Obedience – The Pathway to
                 God's Blessings 99

Chapter 7:   "F" Is for Focus – The Victory Is Already Won ..116

Chapter 8:   Focusing on Christ Led Me to a Career 138

Chapter 9:   "T" Is for Trust 148

Chapter 10:   The Fruit of the Spirit 171

Chapter 11:	"I" Is for Inspire and Intercede	199
Chapter 12:	"M" Is for Meditate	213
Chapter 13:	"E" Is for Energized	224
Conclusion		235
Epilogue:	Brokenness Caused Me to Write This Book	247
Appendix 1:	Suggested Reading	255
Appendix 2:	Application of Matthew 17:14-20	257
Appendix 3:	There Is Hope	263
Bibliography		267

Preface
You Are Not Alone!

Instead of waiting to the end of this book to give you the self-help questions, we are going to start right out with them. Read each of the questions below and circle "Yes or No." If you answer "Yes" to any of these questions, tell yourself out loud, "I Am Not Alone." Though you do not understand why you are doing this yet, just do it. When you get to the end of this section you will know why you are doing it.

Insecure? Feel like no one cares? **Yes or No**

Sick and tired of sickness and suffering? **Yes or No**

Run away from home? **Yes or No**

Domestic abuse, divorced, separated or estranged from your spouse, boy/girlfriend, or children? **Yes or No**

It's Proof Time...

Contemplating suicide, giving up on your marriage or just plain giving up on everyone and everything around you? **Yes or No**

Anxious, fearful, and cannot sleep at night? **Yes or No**

Sexual identity confusion, controlled by sexual impulses, held captive by pornography and the actions and emotional distress it conjures up, or consumed by lustful thoughts? **Yes or No**

Cannot find a job, fired from your job, downsized, demoted or forced to retire from a job, underqualified for a job, or overqualified for a job? **Yes or No**

Home foreclosure, behind on mortgage, unpaid taxes, and mounting bills? **Yes or No**

Overweight and cannot control your eating? **Yes or No**

Depressed, hopeless, helpless, aimless, and directionless? **Yes or No**

Dealing with the pain of rape, incest, infidelity, and/or broken trusts? **Yes or No**

Cocaine, crack, methamphetamine, heroin, marijuana, Vicodin, Oxycodone, Xanax, Valium, illegal or legal, illegitimate or legitimate prescription, self-prescribed or "copped," self-induced or "forced?" **Yes or No**

You and/or your family affected by someone else's use of drugs and/or alcohol? **Yes or No**

Losing hope, strength, and joy because you are daily living with one who is mentally or physically challenged, a sick or dying child, parent, friend, spouse or family member? **Yes or No**

Dealing with the death of a child, parent, friend, spouse or family member by a drunken driver, gun violence, gang violence, robbery or any manner of stealing, killing, and destroying of your quality of life? **Yes or No**

Adopted or born into a family, but not quite sure why you do not feel loved? **Yes or No**

Rebellious children or parents that just do not understand you? **Yes or No**

Are you behind bars in jail, separated from loved ones? **Yes or No**

Do you feel like you have messed up your life, disappointed others, but would do anything for another chance? **Yes or No**

Do you feel tormented by Satan and the demons in your life? **Yes or No**

Is there anything you are struggling with that you just cannot seem to shake off? You just cannot seem to put *it out of your mind and behind you so you can move on. You just cannot quite get over the hump. Just when you seem to be making progress and taking two steps forward, you find yourself starting all over again, but even deeper in the hole than when you began.* **Yes or No**

Are you doing quite well and none of the aforementioned issues are anywhere in your life, but you still desire to grow stronger and reach your full potential, living out the best that God desires for you? **Yes or No**

You are not alone!

If you answered *yes* to any of these questions, know that while this life is at times filled with hurt, sorrow and disappointment, it does not have to stay that way. Even when it is prolonged, you can be filled with joy and have peace. There is a way and I have found it.

Yes, I will help you find it, too!

*These things I have spoken to you, that **in Me you may have peace**. In the world you will have tribulation; but be of good cheer, I have overcome the world.* (John 16:33 emphasis added)

Island of Bora Bora May, 2014

Introduction
Yes, I Will Help You

Do you feel there has to be more to life than how you are presently living? Is there something missing in your life and your present plan? If you are like me, you have tried so many other things and none of them have worked. I am so excited to share this God revealed word with you, especially if you answered yes to any of the previous questions.

Whatever race, creed or religion you or your family claim or do not claim, in your heart you know that there is a God. You may deny it with your mouth and perhaps think you have fooled your mind, but in your heart you know the truth—there is a God. God, in his love for mankind, reveals just what wonderful peaceful plans he has in store for us if we allow him to be the center of our lives.

Regardless of what you are facing, where you were born, what you have been taught in the past, or whatever horrendous things you think you have done, God has a promise for you:

*For I know the thoughts that I think toward you, says the LORD, thoughts of **peace** and not of evil, to give you a **future** and a **hope**. Then you will call upon me and go and pray to me, and I will listen to you and you will seek me and find me, when you search for me with all your heart.* (Jeremiah 29:11-13 emphasis added)

ANDRE MICKEL IN JERUSALEM, ISRAEL, JULY 2014

No matter what you are dealing with, the God who created everything and who is in control of everything has thoughts of peace for your life and wants to give you a wonderful future filled with hope. Even in the middle of what might be the worst possible situation in your life, he says that all you have to do is call out to him and he will hear you. God wants to save you from whatever is harming you right now in this life. He also wants to save you so you can live with him in heaven forever when you pass from this life into the next life.

Just imagine having joy and peace in your heart no matter what is going on in your life. You can have this starting today and it is a free gift. You do not have to earn a right to it. You do not have to get yourself together first. You do not have to figure anything out first. All you have to do to begin this wonderful new peace filled, joyful life is realize God has made a way for you through his Son, Jesus.

If you answered *yes* to any of the preceding questions, then you know you are in need of help. You have nothing to lose by trying Jesus, but you do have everything to gain. This is the day of your new life; tomorrow is not promised and may be too late. Those who reject the free gift of God through Jesus, reject the peace of God and reject living in heaven after death. Do not miss out on this wonderful gift from God. Think about all the other things you have tried and none are bringing you the peace that you seek. Go ahead. Sincerely call out to God and repeat the prayer below. Watch how he will transform your life into a new and vibrant life full of joy and peace that you can never begin to imagine.

Whoever calls on the name of the Lord and accepts Jesus as the perfect sacrifice for their sins will be saved or rescued by God. It does not matter what sins you have committed. Everyone has sinned and is in danger of the penalty of being forever separated from God and condemned to a peace-less life now and in hell later. To God there are no big sins and little sins. Sin is sin and carries this stiff penalty unless you accept his free gift of Jesus Christ.

Call out to God and say out loud right now:

God help me. I know I am a sinner and have done wrong things. I am sorry for the sins and wrongs I have done. I thank you that Jesus died on the cross to pay the penalty for my sins and wrongs, and I accept that free gift right now. I ask you, Jesus to be in complete charge of my life. I ask you, Jesus to come in and fill my heart so that nothing will ever be missing and I can have your lasting peace. Amen.

If you just prayed that prayer then you have accepted Jesus Christ as your very own personal Savior. He is the one who is saying to you, "You are not alone. Yes, I will help you."

Now, find a Jesus-centered, Bible-believing church that has Bible study groups who meet regularly, tell someone that you have just accepted Jesus as your Savior, and you are ready to experience the peace that only Jesus can bring into your life. Find a Bible and start reading in the book of John located in the New Testament, and by all means continue reading this book. I would love to hear from you and find out just how God has touched your life. You may email me at andre.mickel@case.edu.

May I also suggest a wonderful daily devotional book series written by Sue Piper and Sandy Petty, *God Whispers,* available directly from the authors @ sandpiper1122@gmail.com or from most major book publishers. For more about these books see Appendix 1 at the end of this book.

Island of Bora Bora in the South Pacific Ocean. May 2014

Chapter 1
Where Is Your Proof?

They profess to know God, but they deny him by their actions. They are detestable, disobedient, unfit for any good work. (Titus 1:16 NRSV)

Do you profess faith in Christ Jesus and say you believe the word of God, then where is the proof of this in your real life? What do your unsaved loved ones see as evidence of your faith in your everyday life? Is your life a stumbling block in their path toward Jesus?

You say every word of the Bible is the true and is the inspired word of God, but where in your life is your proof that you really know and believe it? How can you put actions to God's word if you have not studied it thoroughly? How will others see the benefits of serving God and choosing his ways over the ways of the world if you pick and choose which words you believe and obey and which ones you do not?

If you say you are standing on the promises of God, where is your proof? God promises that he would never leave you or forsake you in Hebrews 13:5, yet you say you feel all alone and wonder where God is in all of this. God promises you peace in John 14:27, but you are in turmoil and cannot eat or sleep.

You declare you are a believer in the power of Jesus Christ, but are you living a joyful, anxious-less, and mightily courageous life even during the tribulations that Jesus forewarned you of and told you he has already overcome (John 16:33)? Are you really anxious for nothing as it says in Philippians 4:6? Do you really never worry about tomorrow like Jesus instructed his disciples to do in Matthew 6:34? Do you make it a point to count it all joy when you face various trials as declared in James 1:2? If you compare what you say to what you do, which way would the scales tip?

Our words and our resulting actions are what the world hears and sees.

Take a moment and think about the words you speak versus the actions you take. You see our words and our resulting actions are what the world hears and sees. Jesus said what is in the heart of man is what comes out of his mouth (Matthew 12:34). James declared without action, our faith is not really faith at all (James 2:14-26). It does not take a skilled detective to figure out where most of us stand. All we have to do is listen to the way someone talks and then watch what they actually do.

Are you like so many who are quick to make excuses for why you cannot or will not do what you know the word of God tells you to do? How often do you flippantly use the excuse, "I am just not there yet"? How about, "I know the word of God tells me to love my neighbors, **but** you do not know how much these people get on my nerves. I am just not there yet." Maybe yours is, "I know the word of God tells me to love my wife as Christ loved the church, **but** you do not have to deal with that woman's issues every day like I do, so I am not there yet." What about, "I know the word of God tells me to teach, encourage, and train the younger woman to love their husbands (Titus 2:3-4), **but** these sorry excuses for husbands nowadays are so undeserving of any affection or respect, I am just not there yet."

Beep, Beep, Beep…News Flash—You never will be there by yourself, on your own accord or in your own strength. God never asked you to do anything in your own power. God never requires any of us to do something he has not personally prepared you and me to be able to do. What God promised is you can do all things through Christ (Philippians 4:13), not you can do all things through you. So the next time you are tempted to rationalize your disobedience (that is what it really is) by pathetically chuckling, "I am just not there yet," instead declare, "I am there because the Bible proclaims I can do all things through Christ who strengthens me." Then make your actions line up with your words. Take a step of faith and believe God will make a way to do all the things he has called you to do.

Do Not Get Stuck in the Devil's Ditch of "D's"

If you are ready to declare by faith, "I can and will do all things through Christ," then it is proof-time because "faith without works is dead" declares James 2:26.

To say that you believe and never act on what you believe is simply un-belief.

What good does it do you to say you believe the word of the sovereign God of the universe, who has sealed every promise with the shed blood of his son Jesus, and never bother to claim one promise? What good does it do you to have a need and have a check for the amount of money needed to fulfill that need, yet never bother to cash the check? While this does not make rational sense, this is just what we do when we refuse to take God at his word.

We get stuck in the *devil's ditch of "d's"* when our *disbelief,* our *disobedience,* and our spiritual *dysfunction* cause us to choose to remain *discontented* and *destitute.* We even say things like the devil made me do it. The devil cannot make you jump into that ditch or stay there if you already have taken the plunge.

God provided a way out long before the tribulation even touched your life. You could be **d**iscovering the **d**estiny and **d**esires that God has **d**ictated for your life through the **d**eed that he signed, sealed, and **d**elivered by the **d**eath, burial and resurrection of his Son and your redeemer, Jesus the Christ. Why would anyone choose to remain in the devil's ditch of "d's" when every person who has accepted Jesus as Lord and Savior has the map to a better life sitting there on the table waiting for them to pick it up? Have you left that map on the table?

When times get hard and tribulation roars in your face like a raging lion, what proof will the world see that you are a child of the King of kings? Will they see that you believe Jesus has already overcome anything the world may throw at you? If they see you wallowing in the devil's ditch of "d's," why would they want to choose Jesus and serve the God you are professing to believe in? They need to see what they hear you say you believe by the way you live your life, especially during times of trials and tribulation.

PLAYA DEL CARMEN, MEXICO

Action Steps

It is time to get your words to match up with the word of God and then put action to your words. To say that you believe and never act on what you believe is simply un-belief. Take to heart Hebrews 3:15-19.

> *Today, if you will hear His voice, do not harden your hearts as inthe rebellion. For who, having heard, rebelled? Indeed, was it not all who came out of Egypt,*

*led by Moses? Now with whom was He angry forty years? Was it not with those who sinned, whose corpses fell in the wilderness? And to whom did He swear that **they would not enter His rest**, but to those who did not obey? So we see that they could not enter in because of **unbelief**.* (Hebrews 3:15-19 emphasis added)

Start by taking a few moments and think about the words you speak versus the actions you take. Remember your words and resulting actions are what the world hears and sees. Stick a small note pad in your pocket and every time you make a statement about a situation today, write it down. Be honest with yourself and write it down exactly as you said it, not the way you would have liked to have said or meant to say it. At the end of the day, go back over your list and ask yourself the following questions:

What belief did I convey by what I said?

Did my actions validate this belief or prove I really did not believe what I said?

IT'S PROOF TIME...

So what message did I really send to those who heard my statement of belief?

How will I word it differently the next time?

Read Philippians 4:6 and then ask yourself:

Do I believe this scripture is for me?

Do my actions line up with my belief?

What do I need to change so that my life lines up with my belief in this scripture?

Read Matthew 6:34 and then ask yourself:

Do I believe this scripture is for me?

Do my actions line up with my belief?

What do I need to change so that my life lines up with my belief in this scripture?

Read James 1:2-6 and then ask yourself:

Do I believe this scripture passage is for me?

Do my actions line up with my belief?

What do I need to change so that my life lines up with my belief in this scripture passage?

Write out and then read out loud your declaration based on what you learned in this chapter, and then spend time in prayer asking God how you can live your life exemplifying your declaration.

Chapter 2
It Is P.R.O.O.F. T.I.M.E.

Then He said to the disciples, "It is impossible that no offenses should come, but woe to him through whom they do come! It would be better for him if a millstone were hung around his neck, and he were thrown into the sea, than that he should offend one of these little ones. Take heed to yourselves. If your brother sins against you, rebuke him; and if he repents, forgive him. And if he sins against you seven times in a day, and seven times in a day returns to you, saying, 'I repent,' you shall forgive him." And the apostles said to the Lord, "Increase our faith." (Luke 17:1-5)

Trials, Hurts, and Offenses Are Inevitable

When trials, tribulation and offenses come, I must immediately remind myself that because I believe our God is sovereign, nothing takes him by surprise. Therefore, whatever the reason he has allowed this storm in my life, it is **P.R.O.O.F. T.I.M.E.** Instead of getting angry, bitter, fearful or vengeful, I choose this time to be **P.R.O.O.F. T.I.M.E.** My actions are proof that I believe the promises of God even when everything looks hopeless. My actions are proof that I believe, "If God be for me, who can be against me" (Romans 8:31).

My actions are proof that I believe, "All things do work together for the good for those who love him" (Romans 8:28). My actions are proof that I choose to believe, "God will keep me in perfect peace because my mind is stayed on him and I do trust in him" (Isaiah 26:3). My actions are proof of the faith I have in Christ because I refuse to be anxious about anything. My actions are proof that I believe God will honor his word because, "He is not a man that he should lie" (Numbers 23:19). He is a promise keeper and I can depend on him (Hebrews 10:23).

Therefore, when the enemy comes in like a flood, I choose to:

P-praise and pray as my very first response to adversity

R-remember God's past victories, give thanks, confess, and repent

O-obedience, the solution to every problem starts and ends with obedience

O-obedience to God is the sure path to the blessings of God

F-focus on Christ's victory and not the problem

T-trust in the Lord, acknowledge him and he will give direction

I-inspire/encourage/intercede for others going through adversity

M-meditate on God's word specific for the tribulation at hand

E-energize by doing only what God says and waiting on him

Notice how each letter in **P.R.O.O.F. T.I.M.E.** represents an action step as a result of truly believing in the word of God and standing on his word in truth and action. Note also "obedience" is listed twice and is the center of our **P.R.O.O.F**. This is essential. Jesus said that if we love him, we will obey his commandments. Jesus then said the greatest commandment was to love the Lord God with all of our hearts, souls, and minds. The second commandment we are to obey is to love our neighbors as ourselves. The law and prophets hang on these two commands. Essentially he is saying that the word of God really comes down to loving God totally above everything else and loving each other. If we love our Savior, we will be obedient to what he says. Do you love him? **It is P.R.O.O.F. T.I.M.E.**

Playa Del Carmen, Mexico

God Hates Divorce

And this is the second thing you do: You cover the altar of the LORD with tears, with weeping and crying; so He does not regard the offering anymore, nor receive it with goodwill from your hands. Yet you say, "For what reason?" Because the LORD has been witness between you and the wife of your youth, with whom you have dealt treacherously; yet she is your companion and your

> *wife by covenant. But did He not make them one, having a remnant of the Spirit? And why one? He seeks godly offspring. Therefore take heed to your spirit, and let none deal treacherously with the wife of his youth.* **"For the LORD God of Israel says that He hates divorce**, *for it covers one's garment with violence," says the LORD of hosts. "Therefore take heed to your spirit that you do not deal treacherously."* (Malachi 2:13-16 emphasis added)

One of the areas of showing our love for Jesus by obeying God's commands is in the area of divorce. The Pharisees came to Jesus when he was teaching the multitudes and tried to challenge him on this very issue. The exchange between them is recorded in Matthew 19:3-9.

> *The Pharisees also came to Him, testing Him, and saying to Him, "Is it lawful for a man to divorce his wife for just any reason?" And He answered and said to them, "Have you not read that He who made them at the beginning 'made them male and female,' and said, 'For this reason a man shall leave his father and mother and be joined to his wife, and the two shall become one flesh'? So then,*

they are no longer two but one flesh. **Therefore what God has joined together, let not man separate.**" *They said to Him, "Why then did Moses command to give a certificate of divorce, and to put her away?" He said to them, "Moses,* **because of the hardness of your hearts,** *permitted you to divorce your wives,* **but from the beginning it was not so.** *And I say to you, whoever divorces his wife, except for sexual immorality, and marries another, commits adultery; and whoever marries her who is divorced commits adultery."*(emphasis added)

This passage and the one in Malachi very clearly state God's stand on marriage and divorce. Yet in today's world, a divorce is very easy to obtain.

My Story

I can still recall the night four years ago when I was sitting reading my Bible while my oldest son was sitting on the floor next to my bed, doing his homework.

Suddenly out of the blue, he looked up and said, "Daddy, God hates divorce, and if God hates something, you know it is something you should not do."

Now what he could not have possibly known was at that very moment, I was reading Malachi 2:16 that says that very thing. Earlier, the devotional lesson that I had shared with my sons was from Proverbs 6:16-19. I had told the boys that if God hates something you really should not do it, but if it is an abomination like the list of things in Proverbs 6:16-19, then you really, really should not do it. With a slight grin on his face, my son was now turning my own words of wisdom back on me. He knew his mother and I were having marital problems and the word divorce had indeed surfaced in the conversations.

God hates divorce for many reasons. A key reason is because it destroys families and creates a negative ungodly ripple effect that potentially could last for generations. Children subjected to divorce see adversarial relationships, are often used as pawns in the court proceedings, and are forced to live amidst the hatred that often permeates their homes. This example of marriage that is exemplified before them may cause them to reason, "If my earthly father and mother cannot love each other and me enough to keep our family together, why would I think a heavenly Father who I cannot see loves me? Why would God allow this to happen to our family?"

Satan likes and encourages divorce because it can cause many generations to choose ungodly relationships and break fellowship with their heavenly Father. I remember my pastor explaining to my wife and me at our counseling session that as Christians we needed to understand that Satan would love nothing better than for us to be divorced to destroy our Christian witness. Not only our children but many other people were watching to see if we, who very publicly claimed to be followers of Christ Jesus, would submit to God and honor our marriage vows no matter what. Our divorcing could disillusion others on the brink of divorce and further legitimize divorce as a reasonable option even for Christians.

My marriage did end in divorce when my ex-wife decided to leave claiming irreconcilable differences. Though this is accepted as a legal reason for filing for divorce, what it is saying as a Christian is that we do not believe God is capable of taking us through our problems and keeping the marriage intact. We quote the scripture that says, "With men *it is* impossible, but not with God; for with God all things are possible" (Mark 10:27), but then we divorce due to irreconcilable differences. Our actions do not match up with our words.

I have sincerely asked the Lord to forgive me for not always being the godly husband and father he has called me to be, and I do not put all of the blame for my failed marriage on my ex-wife. As a man of God, I must accept my share of blame.

I must also add here that I am not suggesting that there are not times when separation from an abusive relationship may be necessary for the safety of those involved. If you are in a relationship like this, get help immediately.

Divorce was like a painful affliction for me. Going through this painful time in my life led me to implement the concepts of this book, **P.R.O.O.F. T.I.M.E.** as I chose to study God's word and learn his purpose and plan for my life.

> **P- Pray and praise:** "Lord God, help me to embrace and even seize the painful circumstances that I find myself in knowing that you God are perfect, omniscient, and accordingly make no mistakes."

> **R-remember God's past victories**: "Though the fig tree does not blossom, and no fruit is on the vines; though the produce of the olive fails, and the fields

yield no food; though the flock is cut off from the fold, and there is no herd in the stalls, yet I will rejoice in the LORD; I will exult in the God of my salvation. *GOD, the Lord, is my strength; he makes my feet like the feet of a deer, and makes me tread upon the heights*" (Habakkuk 3:17-19 NRSV emphasis added).

O-obedience brings the solution to every problem: "Observe and obey all these words which I command you, that it may go well with you and your children after you forever, when you do what is good and right in the sight of the Lord your God" (Deuteronomy 12:28). I so desired this would not become a generational curse for my children and my children's children.

O-obedience leads to the blessings of God: "Delight yourself also in the LORD, and he shall give you the desires of your heart" (Psalm 37:4). This verse was such an encouragement to me as I walked through the storms in my life.

F-focus on Christ's victory and not the problem: "Thanks be to God, who gives us the victory (making us conquerors) through our Lord Jesus Christ" (1 Corinthians 15:57 AMP).

T-trust in the Lord: "It is better to **trust** in the LORD than to put confidence in man. It is better to trust in the LORD than to put confidence in princes" (Psalm 118: 8-9 emphasis added).

I-inspire/encourage/intercede: "All praise to the God and father of our master, Jesus the messiah. Father of all mercy. God of all healing counsel. *He comes alongside us when we go through hard times, and before you know it, he brings us alongside someone else who is going through hard times so that we can be there for that person* just as God was there for us. We have plenty of hard times that come from following the messiah, but no more so than the good times of his healing comfort—we get a full measure of that, too" (2 Corinthians 1:3-6 MSG emphasis added).

M-meditate on God's word: "Finally, brethren, whatever things are true, whatever things *are* noble, whatever things *are* just, whatever things *are* pure, whatever things *are* lovely, whatever things *are* of good report, if *there is* any virtue and if *there is* anything praiseworthy—**meditate** on these things. The things which you learned and received and heard and saw in me, these do, and the God of peace will be with you" (Philippians 4:8-9 emphasis added).

E-energize by doing God's will and waiting on him: "Have you not known? Have you not heard? The everlasting God, the LORD, the creator of the ends of the earth, neither faints nor is weary. His understanding is unsearchable. He gives power to the weak, and to *those who have* no might he increases strength. Even the youths shall faint and be weary, and the young men shall utterly fall, but those who wait on the LORD shall **renew *their* strength**; they shall mount up with wings like eagles, they shall run and not be weary, they shall walk and not faint" (Isaiah 40:28-31 emphasis added).

After studying these few verses, I have an unshakeable hope and trust that God has a plan to use this painful situation to ultimately bring glory and honor to his name. God has been teaching me what it really means to lean on and trust in him so that I can help and comfort another saint going through a similar circumstance. In fact, God has already given me great opportunity to empathize with, minister to, walk along side, and pray for others in the divorce cycle. So many like me initially cry out, "Why me? Why must my family suffer?"

God showed me how to rejoice in him no matter what. Then I began to ask him how I could bring glory to him through my pain and he has answered. I decided to attend Ashland Seminary, planting God's word in my heart so that I like Paul can be used by God to help and comfort others in and through their suffering. I have a newly found appreciation for Paul's understanding of how his pain and suffering were to be used for the glory and spreading of the gospel of Jesus Christ to the body of Christ for generations since then.

Playa Del Carmen, Mexico. July 2014

Action Steps

When trials, tribulation and offenses come, you must immediately remind yourself God is sovereign and nothing takes him by surprise. Therefore, whatever the reason, he has allowed this storm in your life and it is **P.R.O.O.F. T.I.M.E.** Instead of getting angry, bitter, fearful, or vengeful, choose this time to be **P.R.O.O.F. T.I.M.E.** Begin to make your actions proof that you believe the promises of God even when everything looks hopeless. Use the acronym below to begin this process. Write a sentence under each one that describes how you are implementing this principle in your own life.

P-praise and pray: My first response to my current adversity has been to _____

_____ .

R-remember God's past victories: The last victory God helped me achieve in my life was

_____

_____ .

O-obedience, the solution to my problem starts with obedience so I will obey by _____

_____ .

O-obedience led me to receiving what blessings from God? _____

_____ .

F-focus on Christ's victory and not the problem means I must _____ .

T-trusting in the Lord in my current situation means I need to _____ .

I-inspire/encourage/intercede for others going through adversity. Who do I know that would benefit from hearing my testimony of God's work in my life? _____

M-meditate on God's word specific for the tribulation at hand. I have searched the scriptures and found this is what God says about my situation _____

E-energized by doing only what God says and waiting on him is making Isaiah 40:31 my key scripture for achieving victory in this situation! What does waiting on

God mean to me? How do I know God has spoken to me?

_____

_____ .

Chapter 3
"P" Is for Praise

I will praise you, for I am fearfully and wonderfully made; marvelous are your works, and that my soul knows very well. (Psalm 139:14)

The first response to trial and tribulation, sadness, suffering, affliction, attack, or any adversity should be **praise** that moves directly into worship and prayer without delay. The *Pocket Dictionary of Theological Terms* defines worship as "the act of adoring and praising God that is ascribing worth to God as the one who deserves homage and service."[1] It is of the utmost importance that we acknowledge God deserves our worship under all circumstances. Even if we feel wronged, good, bad or indifferent, God is still God and worthy of all praise. This is not the most natural response for most people, yet it is what God wants from us.

Consider a man in the Bible named Job. He was blameless, upright, feared God, shunned evil, the father of seven sons and three daughters, and considered the greatest of all people in the east (Job 1:1-3). It is clear from the description of Job, he was what one might call a godly man, a good man, or a righteous man. This was a man who was walking in obedience to God. As the story goes, one day God asked Satan what he had been up to lately.

Satan, in his arrogance, challenges God's description of Job, basically saying Job only loved and served God because God had blessed him with so much wealth and family. God then allows Satan to do

---

[1] Stanley J. Grenz, David Guretzki and Cherith Fee Nordling, *Pocket Dictionary of Theological Terms*. (InterVarsity Press: Downers Grove, 1999), 122.

whatever he could to try and get Job to curse God. As a result, Job suffered severe tribulation in every area of his life.

Job Loses His Property and Children

> *Now there was a day when his sons and daughters were eating and drinking wine in their oldest brother's house; and a messenger came to Job and said, "The oxen were plowing and the donkeys feeding beside them, when the Sabeans raided them and took them away—indeed they have killed the servants with the edge of the sword; and I alone have escaped to tell you!" While he was still speaking, another also came and said, "The fire of God fell from heaven and burned up the sheep and the servants, and consumed them; and I alone have escaped to tell you!" While he was still speaking, another also came and said, "The Chaldeans formed three bands, raided the camels and took them away, yes, and killed the servants with the edge of the sword; and I alone have escaped to tell you!" While he was still speaking, another also came and said, "Your sons and daughters*

were eating and drinking wine in their oldest brother's house, and suddenly a great wind came from across the wilderness and struck the four corners of the house, and it fell on the young people, and they are dead; and I alone have escaped to tell you!" Then Job arose, tore his robe, and shaved his head; and he fell to the ground and worshiped. And he said: "Naked I came from my mother's womb, and naked shall I return there. The LORD gave, and the LORD has taken away; blessed be the name of the LORD." In all this Job did not sin nor charge God with wrong. (Job 1:13-22)

Amazingly, after hearing from successive messengers bearing horrendous news, each message getting worse and worse and ending with the death of all of his children, Job's first response to this adversity is seen starting in verse twenty. He got up, tore his robe as a sign of grief, shaved his head, fell to the ground, and began to worship and **praise** God. He acknowledged that he came into this world with nothing and that even if he died with nothing, all that he did have came from the Lord and belonged to the Lord for him to do as he pleased.

Job just lost all that he owned including his beloved children, but instead of cursing God and asking why this happened to him, he takes this as an opportunity to praise God. The final verse of this chapter makes a key point, "Job did not sin nor charge God with wrong." Job endured even more affliction, pain, and even the heart break of his friends and wife turning on him with the same resolve to **praise** and worship the Lord of the universe. The story ends with Job being blessed with twice the riches he had in the beginning and his family restored with seven sons and three daughters. His later life was much more blessed of God than the times before his troubles. God made sure that any pain Job suffered, no matter how great, was but miniscule compared with the later joy he would receive after the trial by fire. Only an awesome and all-powerful God could accomplish that.

Knowing how Job responded to his adversity and how God responded to Job's **praise** and worship during his adversity, we have a model of how we should respond to our trials and tribulations. Immediately begin to **praise** God and express adoration to God alone no matter how bad or awful the news. Usually our first response to adversity is fear, anxiety, anger, resentment or some other potentially negative emotion or response. However, when we consciously make a choice to immediately **praise** the sovereign God of the universe, this takes the focus off our instinct to "flight or fight" with retaliatory resentment.

Do not even let negativity have a chance to take root. Just begin to **praise** the Almighty Father who has complete control and who was not taken by surprise by the attack you now find yourself under. Perhaps you are shocked at where this offense has come from and how or when it has manifested itself in your life. Note that by definition, tragedies are never at a convenient time and we are seldom expecting them. So the next time a sudden storm blows into your life, just begin to praise the God of Abraham, Isaac, and Jacob.

No matter what the circumstance, I personally try to make a conscious effort to say, "I do not know what this trouble is all about, but **you** mighty God know exactly what is going on, so I entrust this all into **your** hands for **you** to do as **you** please. What if anything will **you** have me to do? Until **you** give me an answer, I will praise **you,** God."

I often find myself lying prostrate on my face and clapping my hands above my head in praise to the sovereign God of all flesh for whom nothing is too difficult (Jeremiah 32:27). Often I use the Psalms during this time of praise to God, "I will bless **you** LORD at all times; **your praise** *shall* continually *be* in my mouth" (Psalm 34:1).

Immediate **praise** is the key and it should be continuous. God is worthy of our praise no matter what has happened. Our **praise** is not contingent upon our good fortunes, our happy celebrations, or any human emotions or events. God is still the sovereign God of the universe regardless of what does or does not happen in our lives. Therefore even under the most horrific and distressful circumstances, God is still God. Perhaps our circumstances have changed, but God who never changes is still worthy of our **praise**.

> *Though the cherry trees do not blossom and the strawberries do not ripen, though the apples are worm-eaten and the wheat fields stunted, though the sheep pens are sheepless and the cattle barns empty, I'm singing joyful **praise** to GOD. I'm turning cartwheels of joy to my savior God. Counting on GOD's rule to prevail, I take heart and gain strength. I run like a deer. I feel like I'm king of the mountain.* (Habakkuk 3:17- 19 MSG)

When adversity strikes and we respond in **praise** to God instead of running in fear, retaliating in anger, or murmuring and complaining, God honors our praise and will fight on our behalf. One of my favorite inspiring Old Testament stories comes from 2 Chronicles 20. King Jehoshaphat and all of Judah were faced with a big problem. A large army, more than they could ever hope to defeat, was on its way to destroy them. Knowing that sure destruction was imminent, the King called for a fast to seek the Lord for help.

> *"O Lord God of our fathers, are you not God in heaven, and do you not rule over all the kingdoms of the nations, and in your hand is there not power and might, so that no one is able to withstand you? Are you not our God, who drove out the inhabitants of this land before your people Israel, and gave it to the descendants of Abraham your friend forever?"* (2 Chronicles 20:5 NASB)

Notice he is responding to this attack with **praise** to God. Later he goes on to say:

> *"And now, here are the people of Ammon, Moab, and Mount Seir—whom you would not let Israel invade when they came out of the land of Egypt, but they turned from them and did not destroy them—here they are, rewarding*

*us by coming to throw us out of your possession which you have given us to inherit. O our God, will you not judge them? For we have no power against this great multitude that is coming against us; nor do we know what to do, but our eyes are upon you." Then the spirit of the Lord came upon Jahaziel...as he stood in the assembly. He said, "Listen, all you of Judah and you inhabitants of Jerusalem, and you, King Jehoshaphat. Thus says the LORD to you: '**Do not be afraid** nor dismayed because of this great multitude, for the battle is not yours, but God's. You will not need to fight in this battle. Position yourselves, stand still and see the salvation of the LORD, who is with you, O Judah and Jerusalem.' **Do not fear** or be dismayed; tomorrow go out against them, for the LORD is with you."* (2 Chronicles 20:10-14 NASB emphasis added)

God constantly reminds us throughout his word to not be afraid. It has been said that there are over 365 "fear not's" in the Bible, one for each day of the year. Each time we see one the word is telling us why we should "fear not." God is with us, for us, watching over us, will help us, will never leave us, and cares for us. Hallelujah, we have the victory under his banner. Knowing that fear is a real and a constant threat to man, God loves to remind us that we have no need to fear. After all, if God is for us who can defeat us? We are to be obedient to all God asks of us, then take our positions of **praise,** stand still as we wait upon him, and just watch how he can and will deliver us from what would seem impossible odds. We see this Old Testament "prayer meeting" starting with King Jehoshaphat praising God and ending as the Levites stood up to sing **praises.**

Like these people, our attitude should be that if God said it in his word, then it is a done deal that we can faithfully count on to come to pass.

> *"Hear me, o Judah and you inhabitants of Jerusalem: believe in the LORD your God, and you shall be established; believe his prophets, and you shall prosper." And when he had consulted with the people, he appointed those who should sing to the LORD, and who should **praise** the beauty of holiness, as they went out before the army and were saying, "**Praise** the LORD, for his mercy endures forever."* (2 Chronicles 20:20 NASB emphasis added)

King Jehoshaphat is encouraging his people to believe that God will do what God says he will do and the appropriate response to this is nothing less than **praise**. It could be easily overlooked, but I cannot help but highlight the fact that those appointed to sing **praises** to the Lord went out ahead of the army. They were on the immediate frontline between the enemy and the front of the army of Judah. They were the first responders of sorts. Can we even imagine the faith it took in God to stand between the two opposing armies? Here we see the people of Judah living the principle out that the first response to adversity should be **praise.** If they really believed the word of God to be true (and they obviously did) then why would they not respond with an army led by total **praise?**

OLD CITY JERUSALEM, ISRAEL. JULY 2014

What Is God's Response to such Praise?

> *Now when they began to sing and to **praise**, the LORD set ambushes against the people of Ammon, Moab, and Mount Seir, who had come against Judah; and they were defeated. For the people of Ammon and Moab stood up against the inhabitants of Mount Seir to utterly kill and destroy them. And when they had made an end of the inhabitants of Seir, they helped to destroy one another.*
> (2 Chronicles 20:21-23 NASB emphasis added)

When did the Lord set the ambushes? It was when they began to sing and **praise** that the Lord set ambushes. The faithful expectant **praise** of Judah sparked a cataclysmic response from God resulting in the enemy getting confused, attacking, and self-destructing. When the army of Judah arrived at the scene, the invading army was completely dead. As the Lord had promised, he fought the battle for them and there was no need for them to lift one weapon. Then there was an abundance of spoil.

When Jehoshaphat and his people came to take away their spoil, they found among them an abundance of valuables on the dead bodies, and precious jewelry, which they stripped off for themselves, more than they could carry away; and they were three days gathering the spoil because there was so much. And on the fourth day they assembled in the valley of Berachah, for there they blessed the LORD then they returned back to Jerusalem with joy, for the LORD had made them rejoice over their enemies. So they came to Jerusalem, with stringed instruments and harps and trumpets, to the house of the LORD. And the fear of God was on all the kingdoms of those countries when they heard that the LORD had fought against the enemies of Israel. Then the realm of Jehoshaphat was quiet, for his God gave him rest all around. (2 Chronicles 20:25-30)

Notice that what began as a fear provoking tragedy was circumvented by turning to our trustworthy God and choosing to **praise** him from beginning to end. This resulted in God fighting their battle, bringing them victory, collecting great spoil, and having years of peace as no other country dared fight against the Lord God almighty.

When we are walking in obedience and respond with **praise** to our God during an adverse circumstance, he responds and fights our battles. When it seems like trouble rears its head against us, as we begin to **praise** God we can be sure that our God will even set ambushes if need be, that will confuse, disrupt or cause self-destruction of our adversaries.

Yes, the first response to adversity should always be praise.

While our circumstances may **appear** to change for the worst, our sovereign God is still worthy of all of our **praise** and he is always prepared to bless his obedient children who **praise** him in spite of their adverse circumstances.

CHURCH OF THE HOLY SEPULCHRE, JERUSALEM, ISRAEL. JULY 2014

Action Steps

Just like he fought for the children of Judah and defeated her enemies, God wants to fight for you, but you must surrender to him. You must declare that he alone is your God who is worthy of **praise**.

Whatever your circumstance, all you have to do to begin this wonderful peace-filled life of praise and godly protection is to call out to God and say out loud right now:

God help me. I praise you and ask you alone to provide for my protection from all hurt, harm, and danger. I know I have not always done the right thing and I confess of any wrong doing. I praise you, Lord Jesus, and ask you to protect me, fight for me, and to be in complete charge of my life from now on. I ask you, Jesus, to come in and fill my heart with your great joy and your lasting peace that no one can ever take away. Amen.

Begin reading through the Psalms. Start with the list below. Use them as your daily prayers. Begin keeping a journal to record the ways you see God protect you and fight your battles as you continually praise him. Be prepared to share your testimony of God's protection and love with those God sends across your path.

Psalm 34, Psalm 68, and Psalm 100.

Chapter 4
"R" Is for Remember

Remember to magnify his work, of which men have sung. (Job 36:24)

Instead of thinking that God cannot help you through your present problem, **remember** what God has done for you in the past. **Remember** how he delivered you from the bondage of your last problem. **Remember** how he came through in a way that you would have never imagined. **Remember** how you thought he was never going to deliver you, but in the eleventh hour, and right on time, he delivered you in spectacular form. **Remember** how you thought that perhaps you had drifted too far away from him for him to even want anything to do with you, but the God of grace came through yet again. **Remember** it was the Lord your God who delivered you from being a captive slave and made you a mighty warrior for the kingdom of God. **Remember**, he did it before and he can and will do it again.

Sea of Galilee, Israel. July 2014

Remember, Remember, Remember...

Remember *that the Lord your God led you all the way these forty years in the wilderness, to humble you and test you, to know what was in your heart, whether you would keep his commandments or not.* (Deuteronomy 8:2 emphasis added)

Remember *that you were a slave in the land of Egypt, and the Lord your God redeemed you; therefore I command you this thing today.* (Deuteronomy 15:15 emphasis added)

Remember *the day in which you came out of the land of Egypt all the days of your life.* (Deuteronomy 16:3 emphasis added)

Remember *that you were a slave in Egypt, and you shall be careful to observe these statutes.* (Deuteronomy 16:12 emphasis added)

Remember *the days of old, consider the years of many generations. Ask your father, and he will show you; your elders, and they will tell you.* (Deuteronomy 32:7 emphasis added)

Remember *the word which Moses the servant of the Lord commanded you, saying, "The Lord your God is giving you rest and is giving you this land."* (Joshua 1:13 emphasis added)

Remember *the Lord, great and awesome, and fight for your brethren, your sons, your daughters, your wives, and your houses.* (Nehemiah 4:14 emphasis added)

Some trust in chariots, and some in horses; but we will ***remember*** *the name of the Lord our God.* (Psalm 20:7 emphasis added)

All the ends of the world shall ***remember*** *and turn to the Lord, and all the families of the nations shall worship before you.* (Psalm 22:27 emphasis added)

We are constantly urged by our God to **remember** because he knows how quick we are to forget what he has done for us. We are so quick to forget what those around us do for us, too. People that we can see, touch and speak to every day, yet we still forget or take for granted the goodness we have been shown.

We are warned in Deuteronomy 8:11-18 to remember it is God who gives us the power to succeed in life.

> ***Beware that you do not forget the LORD your God*** *by not keeping his commandments lest when you have eaten and are full, and have built beautiful houses and dwell in them; and when your herds and your flocks multiply, and your silver and your gold are multiplied, and all that you have is multiplied; when your heart is lifted up, and you forget the LORD your God who brought you out of the land of Egypt, from the house of bondage; who led you through that great and terrible wilderness, in which were fiery serpents and scorpions and thirsty land where there was no water; who brought water for you out of the flinty rock; who fed you in the wilderness with manna, which your fathers did not know, that he might humble you and*

> *that he might test you, to do you good in the end— then you say in your heart, "my power and the might of my hand have gained me this wealth."* **Remember** *the Lord your God, for it is he who gives you power to get wealth that he may establish his covenant which he swore to your fathers, as it is this day.* (emphasis added)

Not only are we quick to forget what God has done, we are often so prideful that we begin to think that we have delivered ourselves from afflictions to paradise. "Look what I did. Look at the degrees I have achieved on my own. Look how much money I have made in the business I have so wisely built. Look at my house that I have a right to use how I want."

Like the apostle Paul in 2 Corinthians 11:16-33 and 12:2-6, I could brag about the things I have achieved and the titles I have accumulated. I have been blessed to have a number of degrees, certifications, and titles. I am president of this, chairman of that, president and chairman of the board of this and that, director of this, leader of that, lead director of this and that. I am called archon, brother, mentor, diplomate, professor, lecturer, deacon, connecting link, I even have a friend who calls me general. However, the only title that matters to me personally is "child of God."

In fact, at one time in the past, all of my official emails started with my chief designation: "child of God." In doing so I was making a statement to the world, that although I am in the world, I must be about my **Father's** business. I represent him.

Ecclesiastes 12:13 is clear, "Fear God and keep his commandments, for this is the whole duty of man" (KJV). I am not a doctor who just happens to be a Christ-follower, I am a Christ-follower whom God has allowed to serve him while being a doctor. The Lord allows me to minister to others through being a doctor, professor, chairman, director, and president. However, my life calling and duty is to be a Christ-follower, fearing God, and keeping his commands.

God has gifted everyone with the ability to do some type of work, but as children of God, we must remember that we are here to bring glory to him.

AKKO, ISRAEL. JULY2014

Someone Is Sitting in My Seat

How blessed we are to glorify God in everything we do. In our jobs, walking down the street, in the grocery store, in our homes and even on a plane when someone is sitting in our seat and nastily refuses to move. I was recently coming back to Cleveland from a meeting of endodontic leaders from around the world in Carlsbad, California. From San Diego, I had a connecting flight through LAX, but unfortunately birds delayed our take off and we landed behind schedule. I **remembered** the first response to a problem is praise so I kept praising the Lord as I ran through the airport with only minutes to spare. I kept saying to myself, "Father God, I am in the middle of your perfect timing and your prefect will."

They told me I would not make it, but my God was with me and I made it. The stewardesses were quite impressed because they knew our flight from San Diego had arrived late, and they knew the distance I had to make up to get there. As I went huffing and puffing down the aisle of the plane, I arrived at my requested window seat only to find another gentleman sitting in my seat with his wife in the middle seat and the aisle seat free. I politely asked him his seat number/letter and gave him mine. I will not repeat his response. I must confess, my initial thought was to make a scene and yell back, but as I looked around, I saw people waiting for my negative response as clearly he was in my seat.

A peace came over me. I **remembered** that the Lord answered my praise and I had made it to the flight just in time. I was just so glad to have made it to my flight. I might have been stranded in the airport for hours waiting for a new flight, but I made it and there was a seat available for me.

I said, "Sir, my boarding pass clearly shows that this is my window seat, but if you would like to sit there, I would be more than happy to let you have that seat."

I kept smiling, said hello to his wife, and asked if she had enough room as I sat down in the remaining seat as if nothing ever happened. They had headsets on the whole flight so I could not really engage them in conversation. However, at every opportunity I smiled and treated them very courteously to the point that I could tell the husband was feeling very badly about his behavior. I was heaping the love of Christ on them in response to the husband's negativity because I **remembered** what God had just done. I **remembered** what Jesus did to save me over two thousand years ago, dying on the cross to pay the penalty for my sins, and providing the free gift of salvation that is available to all who ask for it.

When problems, dilemmas or adversity strikes, praise and then remember...

*I will **remember** the works of the Lord: surely I will **remember** thy wonders of old.* (Psalm 77:11 KJV emphasis added)

*They **remember**ed that God was their rock, and the high God their redeemer.* (Psalm 78:35 KJV emphasis added)

*O my God, my soul is cast down within me: therefore will **I remember** thee from the land of Jordan, and of the Hermonites, from the hill Mizar.* (Psalm 42:6 KJV emphasis added)

***Remember** his marvelous works that he hath done; his wonders, and the judgments of his mouth.* (Psalm 105:5 KJV emphasis added)

***I remember** the days of old; I meditate on all thy works; I muse on the work of thy hands.* (Psalm 143:5 KJV emphasis added)

***Remember** the former things of old: for I am God, and there is none else; I am God, and there is none like me.* (Isaiah 46:9 KJV emphasis added)

*When my soul fainted within me **I remembered** the Lord: and my prayer came in unto thee, into thine holy temple.* (Jonah 2:7 KJV emphasis added)

As we begin to **remember** what God has done for us in the past, we get but a fleeting vision of the fullness of just how much he really cares for us. We will never fully fathom how much he loves us or even why, but thanks be to God we do not have to understand his love. We only need to receive it freely and **remember** continually what he has done already in our lives.

When we are faced with giant size problems or adversaries, as we **remember** how God fought for and delivered us in the past, we should begin to have a new and improved courage swelling deep within us that only comes from knowing a mighty conquering God is standing up inside of us. We can now unflinchingly come against any foe as we **remember** the previous battles in which God himself brought us to victory.

Old City Jerusalem, Israel. July 2014

In 1 Samuel 17:34-51, David was a shepherd boy long before he became the warrior king of Israel. He **remembered** he had been under the anointing of God when he killed a lion and a bear to protect his father's sheep in the past. Now he was faced with the challenge of his life. He was up against the unabashedly verbose adversary Goliath, an uncircumcised Philistine who was blaspheming the God of Israel. David **remembered** God's past victories in his life and defeated the giant Goliath. We, too, must recall God's victories in our lives when we are called to slay ferocious lion-like, insurmountable bear-like, and overwhelming giant Goliath type experiences. As we **remember** God's past victories in our lives we will have the courage to defeat any new giant problem we may have to face, in the name of the Lord of hosts.

AKKO, ISRAEL. CRUSADERS CASTLE, JULY 2014

Remember I Am with You Always

The New Testament book of Matthew ends with Jesus commissioning his disciples, "Go therefore and make disciples of all nations, baptizing them in the name of the father and of the son and of the Holy Spirit, and teaching them to obey everything that I have commanded you. And **remember**, I am with you always, to the end of the age" (Matthew 28:19-20 NRSV emphasis added). Jesus promised to always be with us, and because he has all power, we should be encouraged and empowered to fulfill anything our God asks us to do or to navigate peaceably through any adversity that he has allowed in our lives.

We shall walk in the authority of the risen King Jesus, remember his promises, and stand on them one by one.

When I **remember** what God has done for me, this should lead me to give thanks. When I **remember** what he has done and give thanks, this should lead me to confess my sins and repent. 1 John 1:9 confirms that if I confess my sins, God is faithful and just to forgive and cleanse me. Because he has been so good to me, I want to please him and come before him as a clean vessel, ready and willing to be used for his glory.

The apostle Paul **remembers** how God saved him from a disastrous death in 2 Corinthians 1:10-11, "Instead of trusting in our own strength or wits to get out of it, we were forced to trust God totally—not a bad idea since he's the God who raises the dead. And he did it, rescued us from certain doom. *And* he'll do it again, rescuing us as many times as we need rescuing" (MSG). When we are faced with what appear to be insurmountable odds, we need to **remember** how God has delivered us before and know he can and will deliver us again.

As a child of God, you can depend on a faithful God to always come through for you. It may not be the way you think you want or the way you envision it, but rest assured when you are walking in ways that are pleasing to him, you will be in his perfect timing and his perfect will. In other words, God knows what is best for you and he wants to give you his best. Why settle for anything less?

Action Steps

Like David, you must declare in the face of your adversities and problems saying, *"This day,* (call your problem by name: debt, fear, pain, divorce, sickness, death…), *the Lord will deliver this problem into my hands, and I will strike it down and cut off its head. Problem, you will no longer blaspheme my God in my life by causing me to want to act contrary to his Spirit in me. I come to you, problem, in the name of the Lord of hosts and declare this is the final day of your dominion and hold over me."*

Begin today to daily read his many promises in the Bible and claim them as your own. Write them down so you can remember them whenever you face a trial, tribulation or problem in your life. Start with these suggested verses and then begin to search for your own special promise from God.

Romans 8:37 promises me I am _____

_____

1 Corinthians 10:13 promises God will not _____

_____

John 14:12-14 promises I can do even greater _____

_____

Romans 9:33 promises those who put their trust in God _____

_____

Akko, Israel

CHAPTER 5
"O" IS FOR OBEDIENCE

The Solution to Every Problem

__Observe and obey__ all these words which I command you, that it may go well with you and your children after you forever, when you do what is good and right in the sight of the Lord your God. (Deuteronomy 12:28 emphasis added)

The solution to any problem starts and ends with **obedience**. There can be no godly good solution to any dilemma without godly **obedience**. You may come to some resolution to a problem, but without godly **obedience**, the resolution will not be completely whole or provide lasting peace. It will not be God's best. **Obedience** is always a must in God's agenda. What do I mean by godly **obedience**? Very simply it means follow the word of God in such a way that God is well pleased by your actions. Consider these passages on **obedience**:

> *Oh, that you had **heeded my commandments. Then your peace** would have been like a river, and your righteousness like the waves of the sea. Your descendants also would have been like the sand, and the offspring of your body like the grains of sand; his name would not have been cut off nor destroyed from before me.* (Isaiah 48:18-19 emphasis added)

> *For the children of Israel walked forty years in the wilderness, till all the people who were men of war, who came out of Egypt, were consumed, **because they did not obey the voice of the Lord**—to whom the Lord swore that he*

would not show them the land which the Lord had sworn to their fathers that he would give us, "a land flowing with milk and honey." (Joshua 5:6 emphasis added)

*So Samuel said: "Has the Lord as great delight in burnt offerings and sacrifices, as in **obey**ing the voice of the Lord? Behold, **to obey is better than sacrifice**, and to heed than the fat of rams."* (1 Samuel 15:22 emphasis added)

MANOT, ISRAEL, JULY 2014

IT'S PROOF TIME...

The Obedience of Daniel

Biblical **obedience** involves hearing, trusting, and submitting such that one completely surrenders to the Lord by obeying his word. Let us begin by considering Daniel. Daniel and his friends, having been taken captive from Judah, served in King Nebuchadnezzar of Babylon's palace studying the Chaldean ways. They had purposed in their hearts to live an **obedient** life in God and not defile themselves by eating the king's food. The king, however, had a problem so common even today—insomnia. Apparently, neither sleeping pills nor anything else were helping the king and he was not very happy about it. Since he was the king, his problems were everyone's problems including Daniel.

> *Now in the second year of Nebuchadnezzar's reign, Nebuchadnezzar had dreams; and his spirit was so troubled that his sleep left him. Then the king gave the command to call the magicians, the astrologers, the sorcerers, and the Chaldeans to tell the king his dreams. So they came and stood before the king. And the king said to them, I have had a dream, and my spirit is anxious to know the dream." Then the Chaldeans spoke to the king in Aramaic, "O king, live forever. Tell your*

servants the dream, and we will give the interpretation." The king answered and said to the Chaldeans, "My decision is firm: if you do not make known the dream to me, and its interpretation, you shall be cut in pieces, and your houses shall be made an ash heap it is a difficult thing that the king requests, and there is no other who can tell it to the king except the gods, whose dwelling is not with flesh." For this reason the king was angry and very furious, and gave the command to destroy all the wise men of Babylon. So the decree went out, and they began killing the wise men; and they sought Daniel and his companions, to kill them. Then with counsel and wisdom Daniel answered Arioch, the captain of the king's guard, who had gone out to kill the wise men of Babylon; he answered and said to Arioch the king's captain, "Why is the decree from the king so urgent?" Then Arioch made the decision known to Daniel. So Daniel went in and asked the king to give him time that he might tell the king the interpretation. Then Daniel went to his house, and made the decision known to Hananiah, Mishael, and Azariah, his companions, that they might seek mercies from the God of heaven concerning this secret, so that Daniel and his companions might not perish with the rest of the wise men of Babylon. [19] then the secret was revealed to Daniel in a night vision. So Daniel blessed the God of heaven. Daniel answered and said: "Blessed be the name of God forever and ever, for wisdom and might are his. And he changes the times and the seasons; he removes kings and raises up kings; he gives wisdom to the wise and knowledge to those who have understanding. He reveals deep and secret things; he knows what is in the darkness, and light dwells with him. I thank you and praise you, O God of my fathers; you have given me wisdom and might, and have now made known to me what we asked of you, for you have made known to us the king's demand." (Daniel 2:1-23)

Daniel was able to interpret the king's dream and thus save the lives of the wise men of the kingdom. For this he was promoted and richly rewarded. He was already walking in faithful **obedience** to God before the problem occurred and his first response was to seek the God of heaven for the answer. The solution to this problem started and ended with **obedience.** After God revealed the answer to the king's dream to Daniel, he immediately blessed and praised God, still revealing an **obedient** spirit. Daniel did not immediately have the solution to king's problem, but because of his **obedience** God revealed the solution to Daniel. **Obedience** was a way of life for Daniel and friends.

Like Daniel and his friends, we will seldom have the answers to our dilemmas right away. Hopefully, no one will be killed if we do not come up with the correct solution right away, though it could mean missing a divine appointment with someone God had called us to minister or witness, too.

We would do well to live in obedience to our God.

We may not know exactly what we should be doing to resolve the problem at hand, but we do know at least ten things we should be doing as the center of our lifestyle—the Ten Commandments. Interestingly (or ironically), obeying God by keeping these commandments will probably contribute substantially to resolving most of the problems we have or even negate many of the problems to begin with. God gives us his commandments for our own good. They are meant to give us an abundantly peaceful life by leading us to trust in Christ Jesus.

BANANA BEACH, ISRAEL. JULY 2014

The Obedience of David

David, a man after God's own heart, knew the importance of **obedience** to the Lord as a start to the solution of any problem. At one point, everything he and his men loved was taken away including their wives and children. He was even in danger of being stoned by his own men. How did David handle this? He sought God first. Faithful **obedience** is seeking God's plans and will in times of distress. **Obedience** is inquiring of God before springing ahead into action.

Now it happened, when David and his men came to Ziklag, on the third day, that the Amalekites had invaded the south and Ziklag, attacked Ziklag and burned it with fire, and had taken captive the women and those who were there, from small to great; they did not kill anyone, but carried them away and went their way. So David and his men came to the city, and there it was, burned with fire; and their wives, their sons, and their daughters had been taken captive. Then David and the people who were with him lifted up their voices and wept, until they had no more power to weep. And David's two wives, Ahinoam the Jezreelitess, and Abigail the widow of Nabal the Carmelite, had been taken captive. Now David was greatly distressed, for the people spoke of stoning him, because the soul of all the people was grieved, every man for his sons and his daughters. But David strengthened himself in the L<small>ORD</small> his God. Then David said to Abiathar the priest, Abimelech's son, "Please bring the ephod here to me." And Abiathar brought the ephod to David. So David inquired of the L<small>ORD</small>, saying, "Shall I pursue this troop? Shall I *overtake them?" And he answered him, "Pursue, for you shall surely overtake them and without fail recover all."* (1 Samuel 30:1-7)

David and his men did pursue and did recover all that was taken. In the heat of this atrocious problem, when one could have easily thrown all sanity and rational thought to the side, David knew the solution to the problem started with **obedience** to God. This meant taking the time to ask God before rashly responding to his adversaries. We see the words, "David inquired of the Lord" in other places in scripture as well (2 Samuel 5:23, 21:1), revealing a consistent seeking of the Lord by a man who wanted to live a life pleasing to the Lord. I cannot help but wonder how much better countless situations would have or could have turned out if only those involved had stopped to seek God's will before responding in anger, fear, or ignorance like David did in his adverse situations.

The Disobedience of David

While David may have sought the Lord before acting many times, there were times that even he acted in haste without considering the Lord and the subsequent consequences. Certainly his flesh got the best of him in his destructive, murderous affair with Bathsheba, Uriah the Hittite's wife (2 Samuel 11). His lack of **obedience** led to an affair with this loyal soldier's wife, the subsequent murder of this man to cover up his affair, and a baby would die as part of the punishment. While God is a merciful God who loves us, he will sometimes show his love by chastising us (Hebrews 12:6) to help remind us to walk in **obedience** so he can bless us all over again.

We again see David acting hastily in deciding to number the people of his kingdom in a census.

> *Now Satan stood up against Israel, and moved David to number Israel. So David said to Joab and to the leaders of the people, "go, number Israel from Beersheba to Dan, and bring the number of them to me that I may know it." And Joab answered, "May the LORD make his people a hundred times more than they are. But, my Lord the king, are they not all my Lord's servants? Why then does my Lord require this thing? Why should he be a cause of guilt in Israel?" Nevertheless the king's word prevailed against Joab. Therefore Joab departed and went throughout all Israel and came to Jerusalem.*

*Then Joab gave the sum of the number of the people to David. All Israel had one million one hundred thousand men who drew the sword, and Judah had four hundred and seventy thousand men who drew the sword. But he did not count Levi and Benjamin among them, for the king's word was abominable to Joab. And God was displeased with this thing; therefore he struck Israel. So David said to God, I have sinned greatly, because I have done this thing; but now, I pray, take away the iniquity of your servant, for I have done very foolishly." Then the L*ORD *spoke to gad, David's seer, saying, "Go and tell David, saying, 'thus says the L*ORD*: I offer you three things; choose one of them for yourself, that I may do it to you.'" "So gad came to David and said to him, "Thus says the L*ORD*: 'Choose for yourself, either three years of famine, or three months to be defeated by your foes with the sword of your enemies overtaking you, or else for three days the sword of the L*ORD*—the plague in the land, with the angel of the L*ORD *destroying throughout all the territory of Israel." Now consider what answer I should take back to him who sent me." And David said*

> *to gad, I am in great distress. Please let me fall into the hand of the LORD, for his mercies are very great; but do not let me fall into the hand of man." So the LORD sent a plague upon Israel, and seventy thousand men of Israel fell. And God sent an angel to Jerusalem to destroy it. As he was destroying, the LORD looked and relented of the disaster, and said to the angel who was destroying, "it is enough; now restrain your hand."* (1 Chronicles 21:1-15)

Note David's lack of **obedience** bringing about pain and suffering for not just himself, but also for those in his kingdom. Just as **obedience** can be the solution to our problems and bless those around us, disobedience is usually the start of our problems, and unfortunately those around us may also suffer the consequences of our sin. We see the wonderful trusting heart of David, who having recognized his sin, chooses a punishment which puts he and his kingdom into the hands of God, whom he knew to be a merciful God even in wrath.

Jesus reminds us in John 14:23, "If anyone loves me, he will keep my word; and my father will love him, and we will come to him and make our home with him." When you are obedient, the omnipotent, omniscient, omnipresent problem solver will come to live with you.

The solution to every problem starts and ends with obedience to God.

Nahariya, Israel (Mediterranean). July 2014

Obedience Means Forgiving No Matter What

The solution to conflict that has resulted in hurt feelings due to some offense still begins with **obedience**. This means forgiving no matter what. Matthew 6:14-15 clearly reminds us, "For if you **forgive** men their trespasses, your heavenly father will also **forgive** you, but if you do not **forgive** men their trespasses, neither will your father **forgive** your trespasses" (emphasis added). Now I must confess, like most people, I find it easier to forgive someone who not only seems sincerely contrite for the offense they have committed, but who are also willing to make restitution in whatever way necessary to appease the offended for the wrongdoing.

Notice that the word does not tell us to forgive only if the offender asks for forgiveness. It simply says that if we want our offenses forgiven by God (and we do offend and grieve his Holy Spirit when we sin), then we must forgive those who offend us. One of the hardest lessons I have had to learn was how to forgive offenders who were not sorry, but felt justified in purposely hurting me, and made no bones about it, even after it was revealed that they had acted inappropriately. This brings to mind Proverbs 18:17, "The first to plead his case *seems* right, *until* another comes and examines him" (NASB).

Knowing the pain I felt being falsely accused and prejudged by church folk, I have found it wise to be cautious about judging others at all and certainly to hear both sides and all of the evidence before making any judgment. To do otherwise could cause needless severe harm to relationships. Interestingly, Luke 6:37 connects judging, condemning, and forgiveness in the same verse, "Do not judge, and you will not be judged; do not condemn, and you will not be condemned. Forgive, and you will be forgiven" (NRSV).

Certainly there may be times when judgment may perhaps be necessary. In 1 Corinthians 5, Paul appears to be calling for judgment in the church for incestuous sexual immorality in addition to some other sins. One should, however, exercise caution and ensure that they have done due diligence and gotten all of the necessary information and pertinent facts before judging and certainly condemning (if it is even appropriate for us to ever condemn). One could also consider Jesus' response to the accusers of the woman caught in the very act of adultery:

> *"He who is without sin among you, let him be the first to throw a stone at her." Again he stooped down and wrote on the ground. When they heard it, they began to go out one by one, beginning with the older ones, and he was left alone, and the woman, where she was, in the center of the court. Straightening up, Jesus said to her, "woman, where are they? Did no one condemn you?" She said, "no one, Lord." And Jesus said, I do not*

condemn you, either. Go. From now on sin no more."

(John 8:7-11 NASB)

If our Lord did not condemn this woman who was caught in the act of adultery, we should be cautious when we decide to step out and judge or condemn others. I am not making allowances or excuses for sin as God may certainly deal with us for knowingly accepting, allowing, and/or not dealing with sin in our camp (Joshua 7:1-13).

Finally, considering Matthew 7:1-2 which states, "Do not judge *and* criticize *and* condemn others, so that you may not be judged *and* criticized *and* condemned yourselves. For just as you judge *and* criticize *and* condemn others, you will be judged *and* criticized *and* condemned, and in accordance with the measure you [use to] deal out to others, it will be dealt out again to you" (AMP). If we find ourselves in a circumstance in which we must judge others, we should hold ourselves to the same level of scrutiny as we do others, and only do so if we are walking in an **obedient** spirit of humility before a righteous yet loving God, remembering that he sees all of our flaws, faults, and sins.

Whatever side of the equation we find ourselves, obedience also means forgiveness, no matter what.

We would do well to keep in mind that forgiveness may not always be for the sake of the perpetrator's conscience, as they may or may not care to be forgiven. It will eventually contribute to the victim's ability to let go of the past and move forward (Philippians 3:13).

SEA OF GALILEE, ISRAEL

Action Steps

Do you desire to move forward from this day onward in a peace, freedom, and hope that could only come from an almighty loving

God who desires to clean you up, forgive you of any past actions, and bring about the best possible outcome for any problems in your life? **Obedience** to the word of God is essential to making this a reality.

Consider starting right now by being **obedient** to this word of God written in 1 John 1:9, "If we confess our sins, he is faithful and just to forgive us *our* sins and to cleanse us from all unrighteousness." Right where you are say out loud:

> *Lord Jesus, save me. I have some problems for which I have no answer. I desire the best solution to my problems which can only come by my being obedient to your word. I may not understand it fully, but I trust you to be true to your word in 1 John 1:9, that you will forgive me of all of my sins. So I ask you to clean me up from a dirty past, I confess that I have not been living right. Lord Jesus, I accept the forgiveness that you have provided for me and ask you to be the Lord of my life, giving me a brand new start and providing solutions for my problems. In Jesus name I declare victory today. Amen.*

It's Proof Time...

Nahariya, Israel. July 2014

Chapter 6
"O" Is for Obedience

The Pathway to God's Blessings

Delight yourself also in the LORD, and he shall give you the desires of your heart. (Psalm 37:4)

O**bedience** to God is a sure pathway to the blessings of God. While God is merciful and can choose to withhold his judgment of sin for a time (only he knows how long), continuing in disobedience could lead to your ultimate destruction. Stop, repent, and walk in complete immediate radical obedience. **Obedience** leads to God's best for you. Praise God that we can trust that he knows what is best for us. Disobedience leads to *dis-appointment*. We can never achieve God's best for our lives walking in disobedience. In fact, he may dis-appoint us from a position that he previously appointed us to. Note also that partial **obedience** is really disobedience. It may look like, smell like, and masquerade as **obedience,** but it is a fraud, a counterfeit which is otherwise known as sin. Similarly, delayed **obedience**, is disobedience and sin.

Partial and delayed obedience are really disobedience and can lead to dis-appointment.

Israel-Lebanon Border, July 2014

Saul's Partial Obedience = Disobedience

Consider the story of Saul and King Agag of Amalek:

> *Samuel also said to Saul, "The LORD sent me to anoint you king over his people, over Israel. Now therefore, heed the voice of the words of the LORD. Thus says the LORD of hosts: 'I will punish Amalek for what he did to Israel, how he ambushed him on the way when he came up from Egypt. Now go and attack Amalek, and utterly*

destroy all that they have, and do not spare them. But kill both man and woman, infant and nursing child, ox and sheep, camel and donkey.'" And Saul attacked the Amalekites but Saul and the people spared Agag and the best of the sheep, the oxen, the fatlings, the lambs, and all that was good, and were unwilling to utterly destroy them. But everything despised and worthless, that they utterly destroyed...now the word of the LORD came to Samuel, saying, I greatly regret that I have set up Saul as king, for he has turned back from following me, and has not performed my commandments." And it grieved Samuel, and he cried out to the LORD all night...then Samuel went to Saul, and Saul said to him, "Blessed are you of the LORD. I have performed the commandment of the LORD..." But Samuel said, "What then is this bleating of the sheep in my ears, and the lowing of the oxen which I hear?" And Saul said, "They have brought them from the Amalekites; for the people spared the best of the sheep and the oxen, to sacrifice to the LORD your God; and the rest we have utterly destroyed." Then Samuel said to Saul, "Be quiet. And I will tell you what the LORD said to me last night." And he said to him, "Speak on." So Samuel said, "When you were little in your own eyes, were you not head of the tribes of Israel? And did not the LORD anoint you king over Israel? Now the LORD sent you on a mission, and said, 'Go, and utterly destroy the sinners, the Amalekites, and fight against them until they are consumed.' Why then did you not obey the voice of the LORD? Why did you swoop down on the spoil, and do evil in the sight of the LORD?" And Saul said to Samuel, "But I have obeyed the voice of the LORD, and gone on the mission on which the LORD sent me, and brought back Agag king of Amalek; I have utterlydestroyed the Amalekites. But the people took of the plunder, sheep and oxen, the best of the things which should have been utterly destroyed, to sacrifice to the LORD your God in Gilgal." So Samuel said: "Has the LORD as great delight in burnt offerings and sacrifices, as in obeying the voice of the LORD? Behold, to obey is better than sacrifice, and to heed than the fat of rams. For rebellion is as the sin of witchcraft, and stubbornness is as iniquity and idolatry.

Because you have rejected the word of the LORD, he also has rejected you from being king." Then Saul said to Samuel, I have sinned, for I have transgressed the commandment of the LORD and your words, because I feared the people and obeyed their voice. Now therefore, please pardon my sin, and return with me, that I may worship the LORD." But Samuel said to Saul, I will not return with you, for you have rejected the word of the LORD, and the LORD has rejected you from being king over Israel." And as Samuel turned around to go away, Saul seized the edge of his robe, and it tore. So Samuel said to him, "The LORD has torn the kingdom of Israel from you today, and has given it to a neighbor of yours, who is better than you. And also the strength of Israel will not lie nor relent. For he is not a man that he should relent." Samuel hacked Agag in pieces before the LORD in Gilgal. (1Samuel 15:1-33)

The prophet Samuel, who had previously anointed Saul to be king, was now announcing that the kingdom would be torn from Saul and given to another, David, because of Saul's partial disobedience.

Technically speaking, Saul had not completely disobeyed, yet he had not completely obeyed either. His partial **obedience**, was really disobedience which God saw as a complete disregard of his command to utterly destroy everything associated with the Amalekites. This led to Saul's *dis-appointment* as King of Israel.

What are you in jeopardy of being *dis-appointed* from? Know that **obedience** leads to the blessing of God, whereas continuing in unrepentant disobedience will eventually catch up with you and put you and perhaps those close to you in harm's way.

Obedience brings God's Blessing of Peace

As I have been writing this book and silently meditating alone over the past month, the Lord has revealed to me ways to help encourage others in the face of daily adversity. The Lord has given me and I have availed myself of ample opportunities to use the **P.R.O.O.F. T.I.M.E.** acronym with its corresponding words in obedience to his call. Part of my obedience has been to watch for these divine opportunities.

I was recently blessed and surprised by my Case Western Reserve University endodontic residents (thanks Bernie, Chief Sarah K-The Mac, Major DeV, Carol-Please, Jarid The Jeweler, Long-fellow, Peter The Rock, MO-MO, Panda, and the rest of the Endo crew!), who on my fiftieth birthday serenaded me with guitar in the middle of one of my notoriously intense clinical literature seminars. What really touched me was the note inside the perfect gift they blessed me with—cufflinks. It simply said:

Happy birthday Dr. Mickel

Numbers 6:24-26

Love,

Grad Endo Residents

2013

This means the world to me because they were invoking the Aaronic blessing over me. The blessing from Numbers 6:24-26 says:

The LORD bless you and keep you;
The LORD make his face shine upon you, and be gracious to you;
The LORD lift up his countenance upon you, and give you peace.

What greater blessing is there than the peace of God. You may not have the biggest house on the street, you may not have the nicest car, you may not be wealthy or even have a job, but **obedience** to God can bring a blessing of peace that surpasses all understanding and guards your heart and mind through Christ Jesus (Philippians 4:6-7). Peace in the midst of any storm. Peace during an affliction. Peace during sickness. Peace during what appears to be an insurmountable problem. Peace during warring adversity. Peace during marriage turbulence. Peace during children woes. Peace in death. Peace while seeking direction. When Jesus decrees peace in your life, there is a complete stilling such that all natural order must bow down and obey.

> *Then he (Jesus) arose and rebuked the wind, and said to the sea, "**Peace**, be still." And the wind ceased and there was a great calm. But he said to them, "Why are you so fearful? How is it that you have no faith?" And they feared exceedingly, and said to one another, "Who can this be, that even the wind and the sea obey him."*
> (Mark 4:39-41 emphasis added)

The Hebrew word for peace is *shalom* which is used in the Old Testament to signify well-being in health, prosperity, security, friendship, and even salvation.[2] The apostle Paul refers to the God of peace

---

[2] T .J . Geddert, "Peace," in *Dictionary of Jesus and the Gospels,* ed ., Andrew T . Le Peu (Downers Grove: InterVarsity, 1992), 604 .

in Romans 15:33 and in 16:20 where he encourages the believers to hold on because, "The God of peace will soon crush Satan under your feet." This peace can be defined as a sense of personal wholeness that is apparent in every area of a Christian's life, including in the body of Christ among fellow believers, in their home among family members, and even perhaps among non-believers throughout the world.[3]

Jesus tells his disciples he must leave, but encourages them by telling them the Father will send the Holy Spirit. Then he prays over them saying, "Peace I leave with you; my peace I give to you; not as the world gives do I give to you. Do not let your heart be troubled, nor let it be afraid" (John 14:27).

The peace of God, given as a gift in the power and presence of his Holy Spirit, is right here with us to personally comfort us. As this peace rules our lives even in the midst of a warring society filled with chaos, the world sees our love in spite of hatred being spewed our way that makes them ask how they too can get this sweet peace. What a great opening for the gospel of Jesus Christ to be shared as we are continually obedient to follow the Holy Spirit's leading in each and every situation in life.

---

[3] Richard N. Longenecker, *Galatians: Word Biblical Commentary* (Nashville: Thomas Nelson, 1990), 261.

The Obedience of Joseph

The continued obedience of Joseph in spite of set-backs eventually yields blessings.

When we are obedient, not only does God bless us, others around us are often able to partake of the blessing that overflows from our lives. Consider the story of Joseph, sold by his own brothers to an Ishmaelite caravan headed for Egypt, who then allowed their father Jacob to believe that Joseph was dead:

> *Then they took Joseph's robe, slaughtered a goat, and dipped the robe in the blood. They had the long robe with sleeves taken to their father, and they said, "this we have found; see now whether it is your son's robe or not." He recognized it, and said, "It is my son's robe. A wild animal has devoured him; Joseph is without doubt torn to pieces." Then Jacob tore his garments, and put sackcloth on his loins, and mourned for his son many days. All his sons and all his daughters sought to comfort him; but he refused to be comforted...meanwhile the Midianites had sold him (Joseph) in Egypt to Potiphar,*

one of pharaoh's officials, the captain of the guard. (Genesis 37:23-36 NRSV).

Joseph continued to walk in **obedience** even after being sold into slavery. It would appear that he knew in his heart that the grand dreams that he had one time dreamed would come to pass. He knew that the final outcome would be good. In the meantime, God's blessing was upon him and all who were around him. Because of his **obedience**, the blessing of God flowed from Joseph, now a slave, to even his master.

Now Joseph had been taken down to Egypt. And Potiphar, an officer of pharaoh, captain of the guard, an Egyptian, bought him from the Ishmaelite's who had taken him down there. The LORD was with Joseph, and he was a successful man; and he was in the house of his master the Egyptian. And his master saw that the LORD was with him and that the LORD made all he did to prosper in his hand. So Joseph found favor in his sight, and served him. Then he made him overseer of his house, and all that he had he put under his authority. So it was, from the time that he had made him overseer of his house and all that he had, that

> *the LORD blessed the Egyptian's house for Joseph's sake; and the blessing of the LORD was on all that he had in the house and in the field.* (Genesis 39:1-5)

The story of Joseph does not end there with Joseph living "happily ever after." This same master who made Joseph the overseer over all that he owned, also had a lustful wife who falsely accused Joseph of trying to take advantage of her. This landed the ever **obedient** Joseph in jail. What is worse than being in jail? Being in jail for something you did not nor would not ever even think of doing. However, even in jail we find God giving Joseph favor:

> *Now when his master heard the words of his wife, which she spoke to him, saying, "This is what your slave did to me," his anger burned. So Joseph's master took him and put him into the jail, the place where the king's prisoners were confined; and he was there in the jail. But the LORD was with Joseph and extended kindness to him, and gave him favor in the sight of the chief jailer. The chief jailer committed to Joseph's charge all the prisoners who were in the jail; so that whatever was done there, he*

was responsible for it. The chief jailer did not supervise anything under Joseph's charge because the LORD was with him; and whatever he did, the LORD made to prosper. (Genesis 39:19-23 NASB)

Who could have blamed Joseph for being a bit bitter at this point? Sold into slavery by his brothers and now in jail for something he did not do. I mean really, how much can one man take? How much does God expect us to put up with? Yet we see him continuing to walk **obediently** before the Lord. He knew God was up to something. We, too, can rest assured that when we are walking **obediently** before our Lord Jesus, no matter how dire and dark things may seem, our God is up to something that will be good for us.

I love the words of the King James Bible starting Genesis 40:1, "Then it came to pass..." in other words, some time had passed, but now God was getting ready to do something new. Often times the folks you may meet in prison may not result in the best "networking deals," but even in jail Joseph was in the right place at the right time to meet the right people—the personal baker and butler of the most powerful man on the face of the earth, the King of Egypt.

We often question why God sends us to certain places, but when we are walking in **obedience** we can rest assured that no matter what dark valley of the shadow of death we find ourselves in, our God is with us, our God has allowed this, and our God has a plan to use this for his glory and our good. So instead of panicking, getting resentful, or allowing fear to paralyze us, we are to simply trust God to be God and then rest in his peace.

As a result of this "jail cell networking," Joseph eventually came to interpret a dream of the Pharaoh that resulted in saving Egypt, his own family, the future Israel, and he became the most powerful man in Egypt second only to Pharaoh himself.

Obedience led Joseph from being sold by his own brothers into slavery, to being falsely accused and wrongly put in jail, to living in the palace as a ruler as the second most powerful man in the land. Only an all-knowing God could have orchestrated this script. None of us would have written the story of our lives like this except perhaps the final part of being a ruler. Like any position God may exalt us to, there is a training and proving period that we must embrace and trust that God is using to prepare us. He knows what is best. In Joseph's case (and as is typical in most of our cases) this training period certainly did not happen overnight and was perhaps not completely pleasant, but we can be assured that in

God's perfect timing and according to God's perfect will**, obedience** to God is a sure pathway to the blessings of God.

When you belong to God and walk in obedience to his word, he will take care of any and everything you ever have to face.

Action Steps

Do you want to absolutely know for sure, that even in what seems to be the darkest hours of your life, God will take care of you and will use whatever circumstance you face for your good? You will never be able to fathom just how God could do this, so do not waste any more time trying to figure it out before accepting his promise to do so. Just do it. When you belong to God and walk in obedience to his word, he will take care of any and everything you ever have to face.

If this is something you would love to have in your life, then you can freely receive it by saying out loud right now:

> *King Jesus, I call on you. I need you to direct my life and to take care of my every need. I want to belong to and be obedient to you, Lord Jesus. I confess that I have been disobedient and ask you to forgive me for my disobedience to*

your word. Lord Jesus, you gave up your life and allowed your blood to pour from your body while dying on the cross to pay the price for my sinful disobedience. I accept your act of ransom and receive you right now as my Lord and Savior. I will no longer allow anything or anyone to rule in your place in my life. I declare and announce, by the power of your shed blood, Lord Jesus, my rightful claim to the blessings that you desire for me. In Jesus name, let it be done. Amen.

Determine in your heart today to live all the more obediently in this fallen world, so that others can see your good works and glorify God by deciding to also follow this same Jesus that you obediently serve.

HOLOCAUST MUSEUM, ISRAEL 2014

CHAPTER 7
"F" Is for Focus

The Victory Is Already Won

*The L*ORD *is my strength and my shield; my heart trusted in him, and I am helped.* (Psalm 28:7)

Do not **focus** on the problem, adversity, or trial. Do **focus** on the victory that Jesus has already won for you on the cross:

Victory over the grave.

Victory over hell.

Victory over death.

Victory over Satan.

Focus on Jesus' victory since he has already paid the price for you by his death, burial, and resurrection. It is already done, you have already won. "Thanks be to God, who gives us the victory (making us conquerors) through our Lord Jesus Christ" (1 Corinthians 15:57 AMP).

God Can Defeat Anything

What then shall we say to these things? If God is for us, who can be against us? ...who shall separate us from the love of Christ? Shall tribulation, or distress, or persecution, or famine, or nakedness, or peril, or sword? As it is written: "for your sake we are killed all day long; we are accounted as sheep for the slaughter." Yet in all these things we are more than conquerors through him who loved us. For I am persuaded that neither death nor life, nor angels nor principalities nor powers, nor things present nor things to come, nor height nor depth, nor any other created thing, shall be able to separate us from the love of God which is in Christ Jesus our Lord. (Romans 8:31-39)

Keep your **focus** on Christ's victory, not your seeming defeat or problems. God is always with you, God will always love you, and no one can stand against you and defeat you when you keep your **focus** on him. So stop bowing down before your problems, and in essence telling your problems that they are bigger and mightier than your God. Instead bow down and worship before your God, and acknowledge that he is more powerful and can defeat anything that comes against you. Anything includes ills and bills, hurts that cause pain or worries that drain, fear of loss or an unconscionable boss, children in rebellion or even a teen hellion. There is nothing that our God cannot only fix, but also turn around into something lovely, useful, encouraging, and even holy. What a mighty God we serve!

God Cares for You

Keep your **focus** on Jesus' victory, and cast your cares upon him because he cares for you (1Peter 5:6). He requests that we give him all of our concerns, and he wants to take care of all of our needs. So why hold on to a burden that you can release to the master of the universe who can never fail? Who knows what is best for you? Who only has plans to give you a bright future? Who already knows the outcome? God does!

Keep your **focus** on Jesus' victory and seek God first in everything that you do (Matthew 6:33). When adversity strikes, think God first and claim the victory already done. When things are well, think God first and walk in the victory already done. When you are unsure of the direction you need to go and are living in doubt, think God first, and claim the victory already done. Matthew 6:25-34 tells us not to worry, but to remain **focused** on God.

> *Therefore I say to you, do not worry about your life, what you will eat or what you will drink; nor about your body, what you will put on. Is not life more than food and the body more than clothing? Look at the birds of the air, for they neither sow nor reap nor gather into*

barns; yet your heavenly father feeds them. Are you not of more value than they? Which of you by worrying can add one cubit to his stature? So why do you worry about clothing? Consider the lilies of the field, how they grow: they neither toil nor spin; and yet I say to you that even Solomon in all his glory was not arrayed like one of these. Now if God so clothes the grass of the field, which today is, and tomorrow is thrown into the oven, will he not much more clothe you, o you of little faith? Therefore do not worry, saying, "What shall we eat?" or "What shall we drink?" or "What shall we wear?" For after all these things the gentiles seek. For your heavenly father knows that you need all these things. But seek first the kingdom of God and his righteousness, and all these things shall be added to you. Therefore do not worry about tomorrow, for tomorrow will worry about its own things. Sufficient for the day is its own trouble.

Joshua and Caleb

Nope! Not Obstacles but Promises Every Time

Focus on Jesus' victory by replacing the worry in your heart with wholly seeking God with all of your heart. When you do this, God promises that those true needs that we might often worry about will be taken care of. A great life plan of action would therefore be to never **focus** on the *obstacles*, but **focus** on the *promises* of God. When obstacles come to the forefront, and threaten to keep you from entering God's Promised Land, just say out loud, "Nope." This stands for: "<u>N</u>ot <u>O</u>bstacles but <u>P</u>romises <u>E</u>very time."

This was exactly the mindset of Joshua and Caleb, who were sent by Moses with ten other leaders to spy out the Promised Land that God had already given to the children of Israel. These two servants of the Lord only thought of the promises of God and not the obstacles that hindered their conquering the Promised Land:

> *Now they departed and came back to Moses and Aaron and all the congregation of the children of Israel in the wilderness of Paran, at Kadesh; they brought back word to them and to all the congregation, and showed them the fruit of the land. Then they told him, and said:*

"We went to the land where you sent us. It truly flows with milk and honey, and this is its fruit. Nevertheless the people who dwell in the land are strong; the cities are fortified and very large; moreover we saw the descendants of Anak there. The Amalekites dwell in the land of the south; the Hittites, the Jebusites, and the Amorites dwell in the mountains; and the Canaanites dwell by the sea and along the banks of the Jordan." Then Caleb quieted the people before Moses, and said, "Let us go up at once and take possession, for we are well able to overcome it." But the men who had gone up with him said, "We are not able to go up against the people, for they are stronger than we." And they gave the children of Israel a bad report of the land which they had spied out, saying, "The land through which we have gone as spies is a land that devours its inhabitants, and all the people whom we saw in it are men of great stature. There we saw the giants (the descendants of Anak came from the giants); and we were like grasshoppers in our own sight, and so we were in their sight..." but Joshua the son of Nun and Caleb the son

*of Jephunneh, who were among those who had spied out the land, tore their clothes; and they spoke to all the congregation of the children of Israel, saying: "The land we passed through to spy out is an exceedingly good land. If the LORD delights in us, then he will bring us into this land and give it to us, 'a land which flows with milk and honey.' Only do not rebel against the LORD**, nor fear the people** of the land, for they are our bread; their protection has departed from them, and the LORD is with us.* ***Do not fear them****."* (Numbers 13:26-14:9 emphasis added)

Joshua and Caleb, understanding that God had already won the victory on their behalf, could **focus** on the promises of God and not be deterred or frightened by any giant obstacles. Twice in verse nine they tell the people of God to not have any fear.

Fear of the unknown is often a deal breaking fear that keeps many people of God from entering their respective promised land.

Walking in the center of his perfect will, in accordance with his perfect timing, **focused** on God's promises to provide and his ability to make them come to pass, there is absolutely nothing that he cannot accomplish through and with us.

Keep your focus on Jesus' victory - "That no one should be shaken by these afflictions; for you yourselves know that we are appointed to this" (1 Thessalonians 3:3).

Keep your focus on Jesus' victory - "For I consider that the sufferings of this present time are not worthy to be compared with the glory which shall be revealed in us" (Romans 8:18).

Keep your focus on Jesus' victory - "For our light affliction, which is but for a moment, is working for us a far more exceeding and eternal weight of glory" (2 Corinthians 4:17).

God Alone Deserves the Credit Because Only God Can Fix It

Jesus' finished work on the cross provides victory not only now, but eternally. We are fortunate if we are able to survive to the age of seventy years on this earth, so that means I may be blessed to have twenty more years in this body. Truth be told, the Lord has already blessed me with more than I could ever deserve. Even the pain and suffering I may have had to endure has really been a way of refining me and helping me to learn to lean on and trust in our heavenly Father. It has reminded me that while I thought that I was a "fix it all/problem solving" man, through it all and all along the Lord has been doing all of the work. I was just taking credit. The point always comes in our lives when God will make it clear that he and only he is the "true problem solver."

Typically he reveals this in an adverse circumstance in which no one or nothing is able to fix it. Not your pastor, not your counselor, not the child psychologist, not the psychiatrist, not your physician, not children's services, not the state dental board, not the state attorney general, not the lawyer, not the guardian ad litem, not the judge, not the magistrate, not the deacon board, not your best friend, and not even your prayer partner. Just God and God alone can fix the problem.

He often wants to make sure that it is clear so that no one can even think of taking credit for godly resolution. He eliminates every possibility for help or comfort that does not depend totally on him. The good news in it all is that while we may suffer some pain, he knows the best way to make us more like his Son. Molding us in the image of his Son helps to increasingly prevent us from making the same sorry mistakes that rob us of victory and abundant life on this side of heaven (for the seventy or so years that we may be here on earth). Perhaps more importantly, he prepares us for an even greater reward that lasts an eternity on the heavenly side.

The final score has already been determined: You win 8-28.

Keep your **focus** on the victory that Jesus has already won on your behalf. No matter what the problem, with Jesus as your **focus**, all things will work for your good. The story is not over because in the end you win. The devil may have scored a quick touchdown and a safety (6+2 =8 points in football) in the opening seconds of the game. The game has progressed with you making no noticeable advances and the game clock is running out. The game will soon be over and you still have not scored. This was not the way you expected it to go.

You had been practicing and praying. You had been studying past game films and fasting. You had remained teachable and continued tithing. You had been seeking sound direction and serving. You had been doing all of the things that you thought would ensure victory and that you were so sure that God had called you to do. Yet, you now find yourself retreating, under attack, and seemingly losing a battle that you thought you were so prepared for. You begin to feel demoralized, anxious, distressed, afflicted, perplexed, persecuted, struck down, shaken up, and fearful of losing the championship game of life, with only two minutes left in the game. You are losing, 8-0. Your life is over. This is the end. You begin to feel like a failure and that nothing can possibly help. So why not just give up? Just curse God and die.

Not so fast friend, this is one of Satan's ploys. He strikes fast, uses the most unexpected source, makes you think you are all alone, defeated, and that there is no need to persevere because nothing and no one can help. The apostle Paul had been there and says to us, "We are afflicted in every way, but not crushed; perplexed, but not driven to despair; persecuted, but not forsaken; struck down, but not destroyed; always carrying in the body the death of Jesus, so that the life of Jesus may also be made visible in our bodies" (2 Corinthians 4:5-10 NRSV).

Jesus, who knew the final score before the game was even started, enables you to score four touchdowns and extra points in the final seconds of the game and you win 8-28. Yes, Romans 8:28 says, "All things do work together for the good." Do not focus on your problems, **focus** on Jesus' victory.

You win. Thanks be to God for the victory through Jesus Christ.

What Does God Require of Us?

Regardless of what others may be doing all around you, **focus** on what the Lord requires of you.

With what shall I come before the LORD, *and bow myself before the high God? Shall I come before him with burnt offerings, with calves a year old?*

Will the LORD *be pleased with thousands of rams, ten thousand rivers of oil?*

Shall I give my firstborn for my transgression, the fruit of my body for the sin of my soul? **He has shown you, o man, what is good; and what does the** LORD **require of you but to do justly, to love mercy, and to walk humbly with your God?** *The* LORD'*s voice cries to the city— wisdom shall see your name: "Hear the rod. Who has appointed it? Are there yet the treasures of wickedness in the house of the wicked, and the short measure that is an abomination? Shall I count pure those with the wicked scales, and with the bag of deceitful weights? For her rich men are full of violence, her inhabitants have spoken lies, and their tongue is deceitful in their mouth. Therefore I will also make you sick by striking you, by making you desolate because of your sins. You* *shall eat, but not be satisfied; hunger shall be in your midst. You may carry some away, but shall not save them; and what you do rescue I will give over to the sword. You shall sow, but not reap; you shall tread the olives, but not anoint yourselves with oil; and make sweet wine, but not drink wine. For the statutes of Omri are kept; all the works of Ahab's house are done; and you walk in their counsels, that I may make you a desolation, and your inhabitants a hissing. Therefore you shall bear the reproach of my people."* (Micah 6:6-16 emphasis added)

In Micah 6:6-8, we see what God does and does not require of man. We see first in verses six and seven what really amounts to sarcasm from the people, "Okay God, what can we give you to keep you quiet so we can go on with our lives?" We see no repentance, no brokenness, no contriteness, but instead a bargaining of sorts followed by a series of inappropriate answers that clearly God was not looking for in the manner they were suggesting. After all of this time and they still do not get that God is their faithful father who has patiently walked with them. They think they can buy their way out of their iniquity without any change of heart or even any pretense of a change.

Note that verses six and seven lead up to what God does require in verse eight. Yes, Levitical practice did include burnt offerings and sin offerings. Yes, Solomon upon dedication of the temple did sacrifice thousands of animals before the Lord. Yes, anointing with oil was a customary ritual, but none of these were to be used to bribe, challenge, or mock God. Verses six and seven smack of a cold calculating agenda to **avoid punishment without saying they were sorry.**

God rejects the answers given by the people and through the prophet Micah, gives three basic requirements. "To do justly, to love mercy, and to walk humbly with your God." This is reminiscent of the *shema* from Deuteronomy 6 which says, "You shall love the Lord your God with all your heart, with all your soul, and with all your strength… you shall teach them diligently to your children, and shall talk of them when you sit in your house, when you walk by the way…."

Jesus centuries later further stated that one should love his neighbor as himself, and that all of the law and prophets are summed up therein. Love God first as the first commandment states and then love your neighbor as yourself, and everything else will fall in place. Love is about the heart, not about keeping rules and regulations. As often seen throughout the Old Testament, God always puts relationship before law.

To do justly speaks of God's justice *mispat*. Psalm 82 speaks of caring for those who are unable to care for themselves, even orphans and those who are weak and unable to defend themselves. We are to maintain the rights of the forgotten and those whose voices are often ignored or worse yet, drowned out by the rhetoric of the rich and powerful of our society.

The final piece in this triad of requirements is to "walk humbly." Walking in the Bible refers to our day to day living. When one is walking humbly in ways pleasing to God, they are truly living righteously as opposed to walking in disobedience. In Micah 6:8, Israel is being urged to walk in the way of justice and mercy which is pleasing to God. This walk is to be a "humble" walk. Proverbs 11:2 says that disgrace comes with pride, but wisdom is for the humble, therefore humbleness will bring about wisdom.

In this journey through life, pride and disgrace are walking companions, just as humbleness and wisdom are walking companions. Micah is saying that it would be wise to walk in ways pleasing to God as ordained by God. Unfortunately, Israel had violated these principles and God declares them guilty in his court of law. We can see the righteousness spoken of by Amos, the steadfast love of Hosea, and the humility and faith of Isaiah all bundled in Micah 6:1-8.

As the northern kingdom of Israel had already fallen when this was written, the audience was probably Judah. They were being warned that they were headed for the same destruction as Israel because they had fallen prey to the same sins that brought judgment upon Israel. This is evidenced by references to Ahab (Micah 6:16) who was a wicked king of northern Israel. The same sins and idolatrous attitudes that he promoted in the northern kingdom were now becoming a part of the everyday fabric of Judah. They had forgotten how the God of mercy had delivered them from Egypt, and now God was reminding them of his faithfulness.

Instead of repentance and a grateful thankful heart, they responded with what was rampant in their society. How could they bribe and buy off God? God made it clear that there was no material substance they could give to him to make things right. What he wanted was a broken and contrite heart that wanted to be pleasing to their Father. Since they refused, God would eventually send his "rod," a foreign army to take them into captivity.

While the first part of the book of Micah generally lays out the sins of Judah which show up in their society as abusive treatment of the underclass by the influential, Micah then focuses on the punishment that God is to send. Finally in the end, there is hope of restoration after God's chastisement is complete. In Micah 6, however, the focus is on the breaking of God's covenant by his people in spite of his faithfulness and the resultant punishment.

God clearly tells them he expects his people to be a picture of his holy character in the way that they live both personally and corporately making institutional justice a reality for everyone, from the halls of leadership, to those on the fringe of society who would typically have no voice or representation. Just as God had shown mercy to the children of Israel by redeeming them from Egypt, they were to now show mercy to their neighbors.

They were to walk humbly in the way of God, lovingly and joyfully being obedient just because he was their Father who desired to be in close fellowship with his children.

The sovereign, unchanging God of the universe is still concerned with the absence or lack of justice in the world today. He expects his people to be his ambassadors to the world. The wonderful things that he puts in our hearts like justice, mercy, and godly humility are expected to show up on the outside by the way we live and by the way we love others. The world should know we are his by our love that we share in tangible ways with God's children all around the world.

When we do business, it should be clear that we are accountable to a mighty God above, and therefore keep our ethics above reproach. The way we live our lives should be a living testimony to a risen Savior who is a righteous judge. Those who do not belong to the body of Christ should sense a peace in us that "surpasses all understanding" that they too will crave and even ask how they can receive it. When the redeemed children of God do not display Micah 6:8 to the world, how can we expect the world to desire our God? The world is watching.

"Do justly, love mercy, and walk humbly," let this be our focus, as this is what God requires of us.

Peace comes from Focusing on God

Just as we saw earlier that peace comes from obedience, it is important to note here, that peace also comes from keeping our **focus** on God. Isaiah 26:3 is clear, "You will keep *him* in perfect peace, *whose* mind *is* stayed *on you,* because he trusts in you." I like to personalize this scripture and add my name to it. Put your name in the places indicated as you pray this scripture:

Loving God, I know you will keep me **(insert name)** *in perfect peace, whose mind* **(insert name)** *is stayed on you (loving Lord Jesus), because I* **(insert name)** *trust in you, Lord Jesus.*

Ephesians 2:14 reminds us that Christ is our peace, thus **focusing** on Christ results in perfect peace. When I **focus** my thoughts on Christ, I am reminding myself that he is ever present with me, always working on my behalf, and I never ever need to give in or give up when adversity seems prolonged. Although it may seem as if my prayers are not being answered, and although I may not be seeing immediate results, it is important that I continue to keep my **focus** on Christ. This **focus** gives me peace as I wait for the victory that is already won in the spiritual realm to become apparent in the natural flesh world. Then all can see and behold the splendor of our conquering king Jesus in our lives.

Too often and too soon the people of God lose hope in God answering their prayer, and give up on praying about something that does not come to pass in what they believe is a reasonable amount of time. The Bible encourages us to not give up, especially when we are doing something in line with the will of God. "And let us not **grow weary** while doing good, for in due season we shall reap if we do not lose heart" (Galatians 6:9). "But as for you, brethren, do not grow weary in doing good" (2 Thessalonians 3:13).

There will come a point, and only God knows when that will be, that our well doing will be rewarded. Who knows, one may give up just before the breakthrough comes and miss out on the blessing of God, so keep claiming the victory, keep trusting that the victory is already won, and **focus** on the victory that Jesus has given you.

Action Steps

Time once again to ask yourself some very important questions. As you answer these honestly, begin to see where you need to **focus** so that you can attain the victory that is already yours. Under any question where you answer yes, write what you are going to do to change this unproductive focus.

Am I suffering needless pain and anxiety instead of turning my worries over to God?

Am I allowing fear of the unknown to keep me from a richness of life that can bring a greater sense of peace and security knowing God has already provided a way out if I will just focus on doing things his way and in his timing?

Am I focusing on the problem instead of the problem-solver?

Am I telling God that my problem is bigger than he is?

Am I trying to attain peace through what man can do for me instead of asking God for his help?

CHAPTER 8

FOCUSING ON CHRIST LED ME TO A CAREER

I recall a time when my **focus** on Christ helped me to navigate through a difficult time. In 1994, as I was completing my endodontic residency at Case Western Reserve University School of Dental Medicine, I was asked by the renowned chairman of our department, Dr. Jefferson J. Jones, to go and give a major lecture for him in New Orleans as he was unable to keep the speaking engagement himself. I felt totally unqualified to give a lecture to the "standing room only" number of doctors from all around the world who would be there.

Since I had been asked to stay on and join the faculty of Case Western Reserve University School of Dental Medicine once I graduated in a few months, the chairman felt that I was more than capable of presenting in his place. What a great honor, but what great pressure as well. They even planned to pay for all of my expenses to go and present the lecture on behalf of our chairman, that is, until I decided that I was not going to join the faculty.

Now all of a sudden, I was told that since I was not going to join the faculty, I would have to pay my own expenses to go to New Orleans to do a favor for the chairman and present a lecture on his behalf. Here I am with no job and still in my residency program, being asked to help out the chairman who was unable to fulfill his commitment, and I would have to pay to help out Case Western Reserve University, one of the nation's top universities.

The chairman came to me and said that he figured now I probably would not keep my word and help out because they were not paying my expenses. However, I told him since I had given my word already that I would help out and give the lecture. He smugly reminded me that since I was no longer joining the faculty, the department would not pay for my flight or my hotel stay either.

It was then when I thought to myself, "Is he just trying to make me renege so that he can accuse me of not being a man of my word?" I took a long deep breath and again told him that I would go because I had given my word to go. I was not sure how I would finance the trip, but I had made up my mind to go. What they did not know was that I felt this strong "call" to go and give the lecture, but not so I could just speak about the latest microsurgical techniques of the 90's. I felt the need to go and say a word for the Lord Jesus.

My wife went with me. We had only been married for two years at the time and had no children. We could afford only the cheapest flight and the cheapest seats with no windows in the back with the flight stewardess. The morning of the flight to New Orleans, everything that could go wrong with the plane did go wrong. After being asked to get on and off of the plane several times for engine problems, we were finally ready to take off.

By this time my wife was absolutely terrified and said that we should get off the plane because of all of the problems. Uncharacteristically peacefully because I am generally a nervous flyer, I told her, "Do not worry, I am sure we will arrive safely because I am going to say a word for the Lord."

Just then the pilot announced yet another problem. The fuel gauge was not working properly and the only way to know how much fuel was on the plane was to empty it all off and put on a known quantity. Now my wife was frantic about getting off of this plane. Now I would normally agree given the problems, but I reminded her again that I was going to say a word for the Lord so we had nothing to fear.

We finally took off and all was well until we got near New Orleans. The stewardess came running frantically back to her seat next to me, slammed on her seat belt, and announced, "The last plane that tried to land did not make it because of the horrendous storm."

Before I could even ask what she meant by the last flight did not make it, my wife went into a frantic rendition of the 23rd Psalm while yelling at me that we should have gotten off of that plane when we had the chance. If that was not bad enough, the pilot also announced that the last plane did not make it so we would have to fly to Baton Rouge and land there. I promptly tried to calm my wife by agreeing it made sense to land in Baton Rouge, then make our way back over to New Orleans by land to reach our hotel destination.

I no sooner got those encouraging words out of my mouth when the pilot came back on and said we cannot go to Baton Rouge because we do not have enough fuel. Now I must admit I was a bit concerned because I thought they had fixed the fuel problem and really felt they were giving the passengers way too much information. We would have to try and land in New Orleans in spite of the last plane not making it (whatever that meant). I again told my wife to not be afraid. We would land safely because I was going to say a word for the Lord.

We were told to brace for a possible crash landing. We had no windows so we could see nothing. We were blind. We held on intently, waiting for the plane to start its rocky descent through the raging storm. Nothing is more frightening than being on a plane that is trying to land in a flight-cancelling tropical storm. Yes, I prayed, but my **focus** was still on the fact that I knew God had sent me to this conference to speak on behalf of Jesus.

Next came the most miraculous thing. We heard a loud thump—the wheels of the plane landing squarely on the ground. We did not even feel the plane descending. It was as if God held the plane in his palms and laid it down on the ground. I looked at my wife who had the most incredulous expression on her face and told her that we were safely on the ground. That landing, to this date, was the smoothest landing we have ever experienced.

Now she looked at me and said in her most serious voice, "You better go say a mighty word for the Lord."

Not only did I say a word for the Lord as I planned, but I also gave one of the best lectures ever in the history of that meeting. Because of that one lecture, I have since been invited all around the world to lecture and discovered a gift to teach that the Lord had given me. I never stopped speaking kindly and respectfully to the chairman. Not only was he shocked that I still went and lectured for him, we then became the best of friends and he became my mentor, biggest supporter, and like a father to me. One year later, I did join the faculty of Case Western and became the youngest and first African American in the world to become a post-doctorate residency program director of an endodontic residency, and now I am the chairman of that same department.

Who would have thought that going to give a lecture, when I had every reason not to go would lead to where I am today. Only an awesome all-knowing God. I had every reason not to go and give that lecture. However, because I felt a "call" to go and say a word for the Lord to health care professionals who certainly did not expect that at a professional meeting, the Lord revealed a gift that I did not know I had. God has now immensely blessed me to be able to share the love of Christ with people from all around the world as they come here to study at Case Western Reserve University, and he has given me the opportunity to travel around the world lecturing in my specialty of endodontics.

God prepared me to use my university teaching and lecturing skills to teach his word, which may have been his whole purpose from the beginning. I kept my **focus** on Christ and trying to please him instead of nursing any anger or resentment that could have taken root given the circumstances. Because of this, I received a lasting blessing that could have been easily missed. I had every earthly right to change my mind and not go and present the lecture. Who could have blamed me? However, I **focused** on honoring God and doing this job as unto the Lord and not man. I **focused** on the victory that Jesus had already won for me.

Colossians 3:17 exhorts, "And whatever you do in word or deed, *do* all in the name of the Lord Jesus, giving thanks to God the father through him." The Amplified Bible continues in Colossians 3:23-25, "Work willingly at whatever you do, as though you were working for the Lord rather than for people. Remember that the Lord will give you an inheritance as your reward, and that the master you are serving is Christ. But if you do what is wrong, you will be paid back for the wrong you have done. For God has no favorites." I can declare the truth of this word personally.

As a Bible study leader and teacher, an ordained deacon, and active in the prayer ministry in my church, I felt the responsibility to be able to better rightly divide the word of God by "studying to show myself approved." Therefore, after thirteen years of post-high school education and after seventeen years of post-doctorate teaching and private practice, the Lord called me to seminary in 2011 for whatever particular ministry he chooses to call me to in the future.

Like the apostle Paul when blinded on the Damascus road, my call is somewhat ambiguous right now. I do not feel called to necessarily be a pastor or start a church, but I do know that I am called to learn as much as I can now, and at the appointed time, the Lord will give my next assignment. Looking at my present circumstances and the calling I am fulfilling right now, I can see how my initial call to service for the Lord (my past) can be understood in light of my present.

In the meantime, like all Christians, I am called to share the hope that we have in Christ, who was born, lived a sinless life, allowed himself to be crucified to pay for the sins of the world, rose from the dead, and who right now, sits at the right hand of God as our advocate. Keep your **focus** on the advocate, not your problems and watch how the Lord will direct your steps to a far higher calling than you could have ever imagined.

Action Steps

Are you tired of the pain and suffering in your life?

Are you spending too many sleepless nights thinking about how to solve all of your problems and yet they only seem to be getting bigger and worse while more and more of your energy is being drained?

Are you thinking of just "giving up" on this life because nothing you do is good enough to bring about the changes you desire?

There is a sure solution to your problems, focus on the victory Jesus has already won, and his victory will become yours in every area of your life.

Say out loud to yourself right now:

Lord Jesus, I declare that your victory is my victory over every problem right now. I cannot fix my problems, and I realize that only you can make everything right. I am sorry for doing those things that I knew even when doing them, were wrong and now accept your victory in my life by claiming you as my Savior and leader. I may not fully understand all that it means, but I accept your death on the cross as payment for my sins and problems so that I may claim all the rights and privileges of the victory that you promise those who keep their focus on you, Lord Jesus. This day I declare that Jesus is my Lord, and my life is forever changed for the good. In Jesus name I pray. Amen.

Begin by reading these scriptures on the victory and strength we have in Jesus. Record the insights God gives you as you read each one.

Psalm 60:12 says with God I will _____ _____.

1 Corinthians 15:54-57 says death _____ _____.

1 John 5:4 tells me this is the _____ _____.

Chapter 9
"T" Is for Trust

*It is better to **trust** in the L*ORD *than to put confidence in man. It is better to trust in the L*ORD *than to put confidence in princes.* (Psalm 118: 8-9)

"T" Is for Trust

It is clear whom we are to **trust**: none but the Lord who alone is always dependable. Having said that, it is my sincere prayer, and should perhaps be the prayer of every believer, that we also as his representatives, be dependable and **trust**worthy. God often uses his children to tangibly work in the lives of others. We must therefore be willing and able vessels God can **trust** to do his will.

We are so quick to **trust** others, but not our sovereign God. How do I know this is true? Ask yourself when you are unsure of something and need advice, how often do you ask God first and then await his answer. Do you call your friends or relatives and get their advice before falling on your face and seeking God's will? Do you even bother to ask God? Even if you do if you are unable to get the answer you want do you seek out others before you accept it as God's answer to you? Worse yet, do you seek the advice of those who are not even believers in our Lord Jesus?

Now do not get me wrong, God's word does tell us, "Without **counsel**, plans go awry, but in the multitude of **counsel**ors they are established" (Proverbs 15:22). Also, "Where *there is* no **counsel**, the people fall; but in the multitude of **counsel**ors *there is* safety" (Proverbs 11:14). But note God's word also says, "There are many plans in a man's heart, nevertheless the Lord's **counsel**—that will stand" (Proverbs 19:21). So if we are to seek counsel, we should seek out mature, trustworthy people of God who are living righteous lives pleasing to God. The important question to ask is not so much, "What do you think about x, y or z?" We should very strategically and prayerfully ask, "What does the word of God say about x, y or z?"

Of course, we should study the word of God on our own and be able to scripturally support any decision we make. God has often put trustworthy vessels in our lives who we can seek counsel from. I thank God for my godly mother, Lovie Ann Mickel who has always sought to please God and not man, and a father Archy Delano Mickel who came to know Jesus for himself. They loved me unconditionally and taught me to the best of their ability. I praise God for two older brothers, Reverend Rudy and Steven Earl who cared for me, coached me, rebuked me, loved me, and even to this day look out for their little brother.

The Lord has given me loving prayer partners and mentors as well (like Mighty Running Man Pastor Bennie, Big brothers Min. Benjamin and Wes, Confirmation Charles, General Greg, Good "Pharisee" Kemo Sabe Myron, Twin brother Rick, Eagle Sam, Organized and Efficient Minister Charles D, The Gentle Warrior Minister Adolphus, The Praying Shahid brothers, Prophetic Dave S, Sincere brother Stan H,

Uncle Eugene, Ashland Advisor Dr. Gilmore, Old Testament Dr. Tim, Hebrew Prof. Dr Paul O, Rev-bro Tucker, Gotta-song-for-it John D, Scare-the-devil- Greg, Attorney-bro Michael, Preacher Man Robert, Thoughtful David H, Barnabas AW, Memory Verse Diche, Missionary Mark, Rhema Word Bill, Warrior-For-The Lord-Jason, Sing-To-Me Dwight, Dress-Me-Jesse, Apostle-Paul-Leonard, Counselor Russ, Sing-To-The-Lord Minister Myron, The Big Arky Minister Nate, Love-the-Lord-Jacob the Dental pianist, 54-Years-Married Walking-Couple Otmar and Rota, University Hospitals Chaplain Harry W, brothers of the Business Men's Life Group, brothers of The Measure of a Man Life Group, Personal-Prayer-Warrior-Sean and Visionary leader Pastor Kevin... SO MANY MORE...you will always get in trouble when trying to mention everyone...love you all named and unnamed.)

These are men who can speak into me things I do not always want to hear, but need to receive. When I think of the nights and hours of prayer in my family room with men from all around the world who were a part of our Thursday night "iron sharpens iron" men's life/prayer/Bible study group, I am in awe of how our almighty God brings people together to encourage, love, and pray for one another. Black and white, Indian and African, city folk and country folk, white collar and blue collar, young and old, married and single came together to seek our Lord's will for our lives. Even though Thursday has always been my busiest and most hectic day of the week, I looked forward to spending every Thursday evening with my brothers as we invite the Holy Spirit to speak to our hearts and help us to become better fathers, husbands, brothers, friends, sons, servants, and men of God.

It was wonderful as we began including my two sons in this time of godly fellowship and prayer. It was important for my two sons to see men of God crying out on behalf of their families, petitioning God in unity for one another, as well as openly worshipping God through prayer, praise, and song. These were men who had made a pact to only speak in line with the word of God any time another brother called for advice or help, and not simply feed ones flesh and tell them what we thought they wanted to hear. It was not about what our wives did or did not do, it was all about what we as men of God should always strive to do to please our holy God, in spite of how others might be behaving. This called for a certain level of **trust** and responsibility that I believe honors our heavenly father.

Heavenly Inside Information

When we are lacking direction and are unsure which way to turn, God gives us a promise to direct us that is conditional upon trusting and acknowledging him alone.

> ***Trust*** *in the* L<small>ORD</small> *with all your heart, and lean not on your own understanding; in all your ways acknowledge him, and he shall direct your paths.* (Proverbs 3:5-6)

One must acknowledge that we know nothing compared to an infinite omniscient God, who knows everything about everybody all of the time. He knows the hearts and minds of all involved no matter what the controversy. God is well aware of the past, present and future, and can be **trusted** to do what is best for all concerned. When we need information about a particular subject, who better to ask than the Creator himself? When we need guidance about the things of this world, who better to ask than the sovereign God who holds the world in the palm of his hand? When we **trust** and acknowledge God, he will even give us inside information that can direct and even save us from harm. Consider this story of Elisha in 2 Kings 6:8-12.

> *When the king of Syria was warring against Israel, after counseling with his servants, he said, in such and such a place shall be my camp. Then the man of God sent to the King of Israel, saying, beware that you pass not such a place, for the Syrians are coming down there. Then the king of Israel sent to the place of which [Elisha] told and warned him; and thus he protected and saved himself there repeatedly. Therefore the mind of the King of Syria was greatly troubled by this thing. He called his servants and said, will you show me who of us is for the king of Israel? One of his servants said, none, my Lord O king; but Elisha, the prophet who is in Israel, tells the King of Israel the words that you speak in your bedchamber. (AMP)*

The King of Syria was so sure that he must have had a spy in his camp. His every move and even what was spoken in the solitude of his bedroom was being revealed to the King of Israel. God was revealing this inside information to his prophet Elisha, who in turn would share the secret Syrian army plans, strategies, and marching orders with the King of Israel. Having received this heavenly revealed inside information, the King of Israel could very strategically place his troops based on where he foreknew the Syrian army would be. The King of Israel had advance notice of his Syrian enemy's plans. This was the greatest spy weapon an army could ask for—advance notice of all enemy movements and armament placements.

God knows in advance what the enemy has planned for us. If we would only **trust** and acknowledge our almighty God, he will direct our paths and guide us out of any danger. Truly, "no weapon formed against you can prosper" (Isaiah 54:17) when we lean on, rely on, and **trust** in a *holy, eternal, omniscient, omnipotent, and omnipresent* God. We shall explore briefly these attributes of God that show us how we can and should always **trust** God and seek him first in each and every situation in our lives.

The Attribute of Holiness

The biblical term "holy" means "to be set apart." It connotes that God is clearly different than and set apart from man. God is purely undefiled and unable to sin or even have sin in his presence. This holiness dictates his right to set apart people, places or things for his own purposes as he chooses.[4]

---

[4] Stanley Grenz et al., *Pocket Dictionary of Theological Terms* (Downers Grove, Illinois: InterVarsity Press, 1990), 60.

Holiness carries with it an idea of not just separation, but also a withdrawal of sorts, in that it is part of God's intrinsic nature but absent from sinful man. The conundrum is that a holy God desires to walk in fellowship with sinful man. The atoning blood of Jesus sanctifies sinful man to then be able to fellowship with our holy God. Exodus 15:11 and 1 Samuel 2:2 remind us that no one is holy like God and no one can compare with him. Jenney states that Yahweh revealed holiness to be one of his most important attributes.[5] After all, where else in the Bible do we see another word referring to God in triplicate as it is in Isaiah 6:3, "Holy, holy, holy is the Lord of hosts; the whole earth is filled with his glory." Goldingay notes that Isaiah's vision of the holy one is not just as holy, but utterly holy, such that this is the only place in the Old Testament that the seraphs come and "burn" Isaiah's mouth to make him clean.[6]

In Revelation 4:8, the living creatures cry out without rest day and night, "Holy, holy, holy, Lord God almighty, who was and is and is to come." This triple *sanctus* is punctuated in its holy magnificence with

---

[5] Timothy P. Jenny, "Holiness," in *Eerdmans Dictionary of the Bible, ed*. David Noel Freedman (Grand Rapids, Michigan: Eerdmans, 2000), 598.

[6] John Goldingay, "*Isaiah,*" in *The New Interpreter's Bible One Volume Commentary,* ed. Beverly Roberts Gaventa and David Petersen (Nashville: Abingdon Press, 2010), 393.

the twenty four elders falling down, joining in the worship, and casting their crowns before the holy one who lives forever and ever.

God does expect us to be holy because he is holy (Leviticus 19:2). Schwartz makes the argument that while God's holiness relates to being separate from creation, man's holiness is related to his designation as God's cleansed property and obedience to God's law.[7] We would do well to walk reverently in all that God has asked us to do in his word. God has not called the church to be judgmental of certain types of sin while ignoring others as we choose to condemn those sins that are not like ours. Instead we are to walk in his perfect love the best we know how. We are his representatives. We are his salt for savoring this earth, and as such, we are holy when we allow the Holy Spirit to lead our blood bought lives in obedience to our holy father.

Personally, this means that I can only be holy and pleasing to God as I daily give my will over to the Holy Spirit and not walk in my flesh, which desires to sin and defile the holiness that a holy God desires for me. Romans 8:8 reminds me that those who are in the flesh cannot please God. As I walk obediently in the spirit, I am thereby pleasing God and walking in his holiness.

---

[7] Baruch J. Schwartz, "*Leviticus,*" in *The New Interpreter's Bible One Volume Commentary*, ed. Beverly Roberts Gaventa and David Petersen (Nashville: Abingdon Press, 2010), 72-73.

The Attribute of Eternal

Grenz notes in his defining of theological terms that eternality belongs only to God because only God has no beginning point or ending point. God lies beyond time and time cannot contain God.[8] McGrath makes commentary on Thomas Aquinas' writings regarding the proofs of God's existence and highlights the conclusions that God is the first cause of everything and is uncaused himself.[9] It is God who created (caused) everything and nothing came before God, for he is everlasting. Holman's notes that not only is God personal and sovereign, but as the covenant Lord, he is also infinite in having every attribute to the highest degree and is not bound by time or space.[10]

God's creation of the universe in Genesis 1 includes the creation of time itself as noted by his separation of the day from the night in verses three through five and his creation of the sun, moon, and stars which serve to mark days and years as seen in verses thirteen and fourteen.[11] Psalm 90 reminds us that throughout every generation from the beginning of time, God alone has been man's dwelling place. Before

---

[8] Grenz et al., *Pocket Dictionary*, 47.

[9] Thomas Aquinas, *"Summa Theologiae,"* in *The Christian Theology Reader,* ed. Alister E. McGrath (West Sussex: Blackwell Publishing, 2011), 13-16.

[10] Steve Wellum, *"God,"* in *Holman Illustrated Bible Dictionary*, ed. Chad Owen Brand, Charles W. Draper, Archie W. England (Nashville: Holman Bible Publishers, 2003), 659-661.

[11] Kathleen S. Nash, *"Time,"* in *Eerdmans Dictionary of the Bible,* 1309-1312.

this universe and the earth and even all its great mountains (which can be seen from outer space) were formed, Psalm 90:2 resounds, "From everlasting to everlasting, you are God."

How long is everlasting to everlasting? It is eternal, timeless, endless, boundless, unlimited, and incomprehensible to the mind of mere man. God is eternal God all by himself. We are of no effect on his being yet he considers us. He is concerned with us. What a mighty God we serve. Infinitely immortal, yet concerned with the mortal. He does not begin or end as we understand time yet we read in Revelation 1:8, "I am the alpha and the omega, the beginning and the end, who is and who was and who is to come, the almighty."

It must be noted that as Jesus is a part of the triune God, the attributes of God the Father are in fact the attributes of God the Son, Jesus as well. In Revelation 22:13 we hear Jesus repeating, "...alpha and omega, beginning and end," but adding, "The first and the last." Caneday suggests that these words are references to Old Testament passages in Isaiah 44:6 and 48:12 where Yahweh pronounced his eternal transcendent greatness saying, "I am the first and the last; besides me there is no God. And who can proclaim as I do?" [12]

---

[12] A.B. Caneday, *"Alpha and Omega"*, in *Eerdmans Dictionary of the Bible, 45.*

Our God is eternally timeless and as Cousar points out, remains beyond any human manipulation. Yet, he notes that we depend on a trustworthy God for faith, obedience, and our hope of salvation.[13] I am reminded of how finite and small I am in light of an eternal God. I am dependent upon an eternal God for my very being. Each day I must remember, this is the day that the Lord has made and just because he has made it, I must choose to rejoice and be glad no matter what the circumstances I am called to face each day.

The church today should be mindful of Psalm 90:12, "So teach us to number our days that we may gain a heart of wisdom." There is hope even for mortal man, but the challenge according to Prinsloo is to "Act wisely, know what to do, and master the art of living."[14] This can only be done by submitting to our eternal God and being diligent to allow all of our decisions to be dependent only upon what he says in his word. In other words, the only way to know what to do is to explicitly follow his instructions for living as outlined in the Bible, and allow the Holy Spirit to reign and rule in our churches and our individual lives.

---

[13] Charles Cousar, *"Romans,"* in *The New Interpreters Bible One volume Commentary*, 781.

[14] Willem S. Prinsloo, *"Psalms,"* in *Eerdmans Commentary on the Bible*, ed. James D. G. Dunn and John W. Rogerson (Grand Rapids, Michigan: Eerdmans, 2003), 408.

This "heart of wisdom" can only come from a God who is all knowing, leading us to the next attribute to be discussed.

The Attribute of Omniscience

Grenz defines omniscience as God knowing all things. Everything that happens is present in God's mind. In fact, he has a direct knowledge of everything, everywhere, at all times.[15] Psalm 147:5 testifies to Gods immeasurable understanding, and wisdom. God is knowledgeable at every moment of everything that ever was, is, or ever will be. The Bible presents his wisdom as "comprehensive, certain, and immediate including things past, present, future, possible as well as actual."[16] No one directs, counsels, teaches, instructs, or shows God the way of understanding (Isaiah 40:13-14).

As he alone is all-knowing, who better to trust and depend on? Leaning on his everlasting arms I rest. As he alone is all-knowing, who better to ask and petition for knowledge, wisdom, and discernment in this uncertain fallen world? I am so glad that I serve an omniscient God who tells me that if I lack wisdom (and I certainly do) all I have to do is ask him and he will give it liberally and without reproach (James 1:5). This is a wonderful mystery and privilege belonging to God's people.

---

[15] Grenz et al., *Pocket Dictionary*, 86

[16] Wellum, *"Nature of God,"* in *Holman*, 660.

The holy, eternal, all-knowing master and Creator of the universe is freely willing to share knowledge with me that only he rightly deserves.

The church should be continuously mindful that God not only knows each of us in a very personal way, but Revelation chapters two and three also reveal God's intimate knowledge of the life and workings of the church and the resultant warnings. Purposefully repetitious, we see the word of God saying, "He who has an ear, let him hear what the spirit says to the churches." The omniscient God of the universe is speaking to the Church today. He is telling us to get things in order— His order.

Ephesians 5:15-20 gives clear instruction for us to walk reverently not as fools, but as wise by making the most of our time while we are still here on this earth. We are exhorted to not be unwise, to do the will of God, to stay filled with the Spirit, to encourage one another, and to give thanks always to God the Father through Jesus his Son. God is all-knowing and as our almighty God, he is also all-powerful and can do anything but fail. This brings us to the next attribute for discussion.

The Attribute of Omnipotence

The definition of omnipotence, per Grenz, refers to God being able to do anything in regard to his divine plans, especially demonstrated as it relates to his overcoming evil for the good. Grenz notes this to have been prominently displayed by Christ being crucified by a rebellious people, for whom his death ironically, paid the price for their sins and provided for their salvation.[17] In his omnipotence, and only as the Almighty could, he used an evil act by an evil people, to ultimately provide the best gift man will ever know, eternal salvation. There is no limit to the all-powerful God. Bond adds, that not only does all power belong to God, but additionally, scripture confirms that "with God, all things are possible" (Matthew 19:26). [18]

Jeremiah 32:27 powerfully proclaims, "Behold, I am the Lord, the God of all flesh, is there anything too hard for me?" The all-powerful God is speaking for himself and letting his people know that he, as ruler and Creator, has all power to use when, and as he sees fit, with absolutely no limitations. God's power is so unfathomable to man that Ephesians 3:20 tells us that God's power even exceeds anything we could ever think to ask for. What joy that brings to my heart, knowing that God loves me so much that he is willing to do even more for me than I am able to ask for in prayer. Even more, he knows exactly what I need as the Holy Spirit intercedes for me when I do not know what to pray (Romans 8:26-27). While God is with me and doing all of this

---

[17] Grenz et al., *Pocket Dictionary*, 85-86.
[18] Steve Bond, *"Omnipotence"* in *Holman*, 1220.

for me, at the same time he is able to be with everyone else and equally exceed their expectations. This brings us to the next attribute of God.

The Attribute of Omnipresence

Grenz defines omnipresence as God's ability to be everywhere at the same time or more appropriately, for everything to be in God's presence at once and therefore within his reach and care.[19] Anything God created is limited to the space it occupies, while God the Creator continues to hold everything together through Jesus (Hebrews 1:3) and is present to all of creation.

In Psalm 139:7-12, David proclaims that there is no place he can go that is not in the presence of God. Whether he is in heaven or hell, or even to the uttermost parts of the sea or darkness, he cannot hide from God's presence. Even though God is omnipresent, he is not always perceived by his creation, but he can surely make his presence felt through his merciful blessings or perhaps even his judgment.[20]

God's presence is not static or passive, but it is a relational presence that is grounded in, and informed by a love that is steadfast and working for the good, even during times of judgment. As heaven is God's throne and the earth is God's footstool, any action of God from

---

[19] Grenz et al., *Pocket Dictionary*, 86.

[20] Bond, "Omnipresence," in *Holman*, 1221

heaven to earth is really just the movement from one part of God's creation to another. God is separated from the world, but in his omnipresence and omnipotence, he "works from within the world, not on the world from without."[21]

Matthew 7:21 warns that not everyone who claims to profess the Lord will enter the kingdom of heaven. The church is always in the presence of God, but the real question is, "Is God present in the church?" While God is a righteous judge, he is also known for the final attribute we will discuss, goodness.

The Attribute of Goodness

God's goodness in the Old Testament was often made manifest by his justice and mercy. His protection and assistance to the fatherless, widows, the disenfranchised, and the marginalized of society was shown to those who feared his name and **trusted** in him (Psalm 31:19). We are told to "taste and see" for ourselves that he is good (Psalm 34:8). The goodness of God is so profound, that even the worst of sinners can have their sins immediately forgiven upon repentance. The truth is, while we try to make distinctions between "our" little sins

---

[21] Terence E. Fretheim, "God as Present and Active," in *The New Interpreter's Dictionary of the Bible, Vol.2*, ed., Katharine Doob Sakenfeld (Nashville, TN.: Abingdon Press, 2007), 611.

versus "their" big sins, to God sin is sin. The fact of the matter is all have sinned and do fall short of God's holy standards (Romans 3:23).

The goodness of God is shown most distinctly in that while we were still God's sinful enemies, he demonstrated great love for us by sacrificing his only Son, Jesus, to pay for his enemies' sins (your sins and mine) and saved us from the wrath we deserved (Romans 5:8-9). Therefore, God's goodness really climaxes in the granting of eternal life with him, to all who believe on Jesus Christ as Lord and Savior, not according to any works of righteousness that we have accomplished, but because of his mercy and grace.[22]

As the church of God, just as God demonstrated his love for us while we were yet sinners, we too ought to imitate God's goodness and concretely show our love in very tangible and life changing meaningful ways even to a hostile world who opposes God and therefore opposes us.

Finally, while I have attempted to draw together some insightful observations that have been used to enable a better understanding of our God throughout the ages, it is intellectually clear that in spite of man's best efforts, God is incomprehensible. We will never be able to completely fathom his immensity. Deuteronomy 29:29 reminds us

---

[22] John Y. H. Yieh, "*Good*," in *The New Interpreter's Dictionary of the Bible, Vol. 2*, 627.

that while we may never know God fully, nevertheless, he created us in his image and gave us his word, which is a revelation of himself. Therefore, although we may not know him fully, we may come to know him truly. Man's finite and oft irrationally narrow speculation about God will never lead us to the knowledge of God that we desire. God's word, however, as revealed in his holy scriptures, must continue to be the basis of any discussion of who God is and what he desires of we his people.[23]

My prayer is that all may come to know, love, worship and serve the holy, eternal, omniscient, omnipotent, omnipresent, and good God in a way that is most pleasing to him.

Trust Tied to Faith

Trust and faith go hand in hand. Faithfulness is one aspect of the fruit of the Holy Spirit. In his classic work entitled *de fide orthodoxa*, John of Damascus writes:

> "In the same way, we believe in the Holy Spirit, the Lord and giver of life, who proceeds from the Father and dwells in the Son; who is adored and glorified

---

[23] Wellum, *"Knowledge of God,"* in *Holman*, 659.

together with the Father and Son as consubstantial and co-eternal with them; who is the true and authoritative Spirit of God and the source of wisdom and life and sanctification; who is God together with the Father and the Son and is proclaimed as such; who is uncreated, complete, creative, almighty, all-working, infinite in power..." [24]

The Holy Spirit is a part of the singular triune Godhead consisting of God, the Father; God, the Son; and God, the Holy Spirit and as such, serves a particular divine function. Augustine, even earlier than John of Damascus, noted that the Holy Spirit has a distinctive role and identity within the trinity and could be thought of as "love."[25]

Let me make it plainly clear that I am **not** speaking of three different gods (polytheistic) as some would suggest of Christianity. I am speaking of one God, (monotheistic) with three distinct godly functions. People have asked me, "How could God rule as three roles in one?" I would answer first because he alone is God and can do anything he chooses whether we understand it or not. But I have in turn

---

[24] John of Damascus, *de fide orthodoxa* in *The Christian Theology Reader*, ed., Alister E. McGrath (West Sussex: Wiley-Blackwell, 2011), 174.

[25] Augustine, *de Trinitae* in *The Christian Theology Reader, 169*

asked, "Why is this three in one concept so objectionable, so unreasonable, and so unbelievable that one would consider this as part of the grounds to reject Jesus as God, the Son? Why is this so far-fetched?" As one earthly father, I serve in a number of roles, functions, and capacities. I am André the father of two boys, André the son of Lovie and Archy, and André the loving husband of my beautiful and talented wife Estomarys. I am also André the brother, André the friend, and André the sinner saved by the grace of God.

God, the Holy Spirit enables Christ-followers (Christians) to participate in and benefit from the death of God, the Son, Christ Jesus on the cross. The apostle Paul notes in Galatians 2:19-20, that when we accept Christ Jesus as our Savior and Lord, our old sinful flesh nature is crucified with Christ and the risen Christ then comes to live in the hearts of each of his new followers. The power that the sinful flesh once had over us, causing us to ignore God and sin, is crucified or destroyed as we are filled with that same Holy Spirit. Because we are filled with the Holy Spirit, there should be a progressively diminishing grip of power that the sinful flesh has over us, accompanied by an ever increasing surge in the outward manifestation of the presence of the Holy Spirit in our lives, known as the Fruit of the Spirit.[26] This fruit is indeed a gift

---

[26] David A. DeSilva, *An Introduction to the New Testament* (Downers Grove: InterVarsity Press, 2004), 520.

of God, given through the Holy Spirit, which results in a change in our quality of life, not by our human efforts, but as directed by the Spirit.[27]

Action Steps

In order to know, love, worship and serve the holy, eternal, omniscient, omnipotent, omnipresent, and good God in a way that is most pleasing to him, we must study to learn more about these amazing attributes of our God. Take the time to review the definitions of each of these attributes and write them out in your own words. Then praise God for the amazing Father he is to you personally.

Holy _____

Eternal _____

Omniscient _____

Omnipotent _____

Omnipresent _____

Good _____

---

[27] Richard N. Longenecker, *Galatians: Word Biblical Commentary* (Nashville: Thomas Nelson, 1990), 259.

Chapter 10
The Fruit of the Spirit

But I say, walk by the spirit, and you will not carry out the desire of the flesh. For the flesh sets its desire against the spirit, and the spirit against the flesh; for these are in opposition to one another, so that you may not do the things that you please. But if you are led by the spirit, you are not under the law. Now the deeds of the flesh are evident, which are: immorality, impurity, sensuality, idolatry, sorcery, enmities, strife, jealousy, outbursts of anger, disputes, dissensions, factions, envying, drunkenness, carousing, and things like these, of which I forewarn you, just as I have forewarned you, that those who practice such things will not inherit the kingdom of God. But the Fruit of the Spirit is love, joy, peace, patience, kindness, goodness, faithfulness, gentleness, and self-control; against such things there is no law. Now those who belong to Christ Jesus have crucified the flesh with its passions and desires. If we live by the spirit, let us also walk by the spirit. Let us not become boastful, challenging one another, envying one another. (Galatians 5:16-26 NASB)

While there are nine aspects or virtues of the fruit, we will presently discuss only three particular aspects of the Fruit of the Spirit by describing or defining each, giving scriptural examples and finally discussing how the Holy Spirit's manifestation of each aspect of this fruit, should define and form our day to day living as Christians. In other words, knowing that the power of the Holy Spirit should be manifested in our lives as noted by the "fruit" that can be seen by those around us, how can we be a light to this sinful dark world and fulfill the commission of making disciples of the world?

The three aspects of the fruit of the Spirit that we will concentrate on are love, faithfulness, and self-control. Ironically, the first two to be considered are also attributes of God. God is love. God is faithful. How wonderful it is to think that God, through his Holy Spirit, has shown his love of man, by gifting us with some of the same attributes that "define" him. When I consider how God wants to have an intimate relationship with man, it is clear he makes every effort to reach out and call each of us by name into his very presence. It is apparent from the above quoted scripture, that while the fruit of the Spirit is a gift that is to be desired, the works of the flesh are not only undesirable, but are set in bold contrast and act as clear inhibitors to entry into the kingdom of God. Barclay expresses just what this "flesh" and its works represent.

> *The flesh is what man has made himself in contrast with man as God made him. The flesh is man as he has allowed himself to become in contrast with man as God meant him to be. The flesh stands for the total effect upon man of his own sin and of the sin of his fathers and of the sin of all men who have gone before him ... the flesh is man as he is apart from Jesus Christ and his Spirit.*[28]

Apart from Christ and the work of the Holy Spirit, we stand no chance of nullifying the flesh and being able to manifest the Fruit of the Spirit in our lives. Jinkins points out an important fact that we would do well to remember, "All that Jesus did, he did resting in the power of the

---

[28] W. Barclay, *Flesh and Spirit: An Examination of Galatians 5:19-23* (London: SCM, 1962), 22.

Spirit rather than in his own creaturely resources."[29] We are hopeless without the Spirit of God which Jesus promised to come and not only comfort us, but guide us in truth. This Spirit which Jesus said would come after he left, was and is God, the Holy Spirit, and therefore has been since the beginning of time, with God the Father and God the Son.

While a number of similar phrases and partial parallels to "Fruit of the Spirit" do exist, this Galatians 5:22 text is the only place where it is seen written in these exact words.[30] Additionally, Beale notes in his article on the Old Testament background of Paul's use of "Fruit of the Spirit," that the fruit metaphor can be seen alluded to even in Isaiah's references to restoration and new Exodus in chapters 32 and 57.[31] Thus, the idea that there were no references to the Holy Spirit, or even Fruit of the Spirit before the New Testament is simply not true.

Fruit of the Spirit: Love

The first aspect of the Fruit that we will consider is love. Grenz defines love, especially *agape* love, as a part of God's essential nature that characterizes God's relationship with man. It is a supernatural

---

[29] Michael Jinkins, *Invitation to Theology* (Downers Grove: InterVarsity, 2001), 196.

[30] Benny C. Aker, "Fruit of the Spirit" in *New interpreter's Dictionary of the Bible, Vol.2*, ed., Katharine Doob Sakenfeld (Nashville, TN.: Abingdon Press, 2007), 492.

[31] G.K. Beale, "The Old Testament Background of Paul's Reference to 'the Fruit of the Spirit' in Galatians 5:22." *Bulletin for Biblical Research* 15 (2005): 4-5.

aspect of God that is reflected in the body of Christ-believers in relation to the Almighty, and among all believers as shaped by the Holy Spirit's presence. Because of this association between love and God's very character, believers have as a central tenet of discipleship, love for one another which includes unconditionally sacrificing themselves and giving preference to others.[32] It is no accident that love is the first mentioned of the Fruit of the Spirit in Galatians 5:22. In Greek structure, the first item mentioned on a list would be the most emphasized. Just a few verses prior in verse thirteen, there was an exhortation, "through love serve one another," which could mean that the other eight listed aspects of the Fruit come about as a result of this love.[33]

After all, or perhaps more correctly first of all, God is love. 1 John 4:7-9 reminds us that not only is God love, but we are to love one another as love is from God, and everyone who loves is born of God and knows God. The love of God was manifested in us. Here we see the gift of God, given first through his Son being given as a ransom for our sins, and later as a result of the Holy Spirit coming to tabernacle with us. Interestingly, Paul's summary of the whole Law in Galatians 5:14 is even shorter than Jesus' summary in Matthew 22: 36-40. Paul

---

[32] Stanley Grenz, David Guretzki and Cherith Fee Nordling, *Pocket Dictionary of Theological Terms*
(Downers Grove, Illinois: InterVarsity Press, 1990), 73-74.

[33] Longenecker, *Galatians,* 260.

noted that one should love his neighbor as himself. Jesus, of course in giving a complete answer to the question of the greatest commandment, said that one should first, love God with all that one has, and secondly, love his neighbor. Jesus does conclude in verse forty, "On these two commandments depend the whole law and the prophets."

The important point is that love is the key to fulfilling all that God has asked us to do. For Paul, Christian love expresses itself in service to others that can only be fulfilled by being grounded and guided by the Spirit of God that fills each new believer in their new walk of life, and their new way of living out *torah* (God's Law) through faith in Jesus Christ alone.[34] Really, the Fruit of the Spirit as far as Paul is concerned is love, and the subsequent eight other aspects of the fruit that follow in the list characterize his understanding of love.[35]

How can any discussion of Paul's writing about love not include 1 Corinthians 13 because without the Holy Spirit, it is humanly impossible to love as expressed hereafter?

> *Love is patient, love is kind…love does not brag…does not act unbecomingly; does not seek its own, is not*

---

[34] ibid, 241.

[35] John Painter, "The Fruit of the Spirit is Love: Galatians 5:22-23, An Exegetical Note." *Journal of Theology for Southern Africa*. (1973): 59

provoked, does not take into account a wrong suffered, does not rejoice in unrighteousness, but rejoices in the truth; bears all things, believes all things, hopes all things, endures all things. Love never fails...but now faith, hope, love, abide these three; but the greatest of these three is love. (1 Corinthians 13:4-13, NASB)

What I find as an amazing fulfillment of God's word, is that each of the nine aspects of the Fruit of the Spirit are in some way, either explicitly or implicitly, revealed in this passage on love in 1 Corinthians 13. Love is clearly represented as the greatest desire we should have. Joy is shown in love rejoicing. Peace is a result of love not acting unbecomingly, seeking its own, and not taking into account a wrong suffered. Love is shown through patience. Love is exemplified through kindness. Goodness is shown as love does not rejoice in unrighteousness. Faithfulness is one of the three abiding aspects of love along with gentleness which endures all things, and finally self-control is not being provoked to react other than in love.

It has been said that what the world needs most is love. I believe that in order for us to fulfill the great commission and make disciples of every nation, people everywhere must see the love in us by our concrete actions, not by our word alone. 1 John 3:18 is clear, "Let us not love in word or tongue, but in deed and truth."

People do not care how much you know or what you know until they know how much you care.

Before we can share the gospel of love (God so loved the world that he sacrificed his son Jesus to die for our sins), we must first simply show love. Without judging, without prejudice, without our Americanized-entitlement presuppositions, and love our neighbors as God first loved us.

The Fence, the Law and Love for My Neighbors

I am reminded of a controversy with my next door neighbors when we moved to a home that had a pretty partially wooded lot attached next door and had a nice football-like field for the boys and me to play our sports. We immediately landscaped the attached lot so as to incorporate it seamlessly into the lot with our home. The lot had somewhat deteriorated over the years prior, so we had to revive the grass, remove old stumps, and even added a number of plantings to enhance the scenery.

Almost immediately upon moving into this fine new neighborhood, we noticed that the neighbors on the other side of the lot would regularly make use of the lot as well. Cookouts, badminton, baseball, they were having a great time using our land, and we really had no problem with that. We just figured that since the lot had been empty for so long, the old owners probably allowed them to use it. No problem.

Then they started going beyond our new attached lot directly onto our home lot, even directly in front of our home to throw their baseball around. We would wave hello and see if they would talk with us, but they would just ignore us. Our boys would speak to them and received nothing in return. We were in shock. We found out later that we were only one of the two African American families in that area, but we had never even thought about that as an issue. I must confess that I was a bit bewildered as I waited for the "right opportunity" to connect with them, but it never came.

Well as it happened, I decided to get a German shepherd dog. One of the men in my Thursday night Bible study was an excellent dog trainer and he found me the perfect pup—Tiberius von Maximus. This was a kingly name for a kingly dog which came right in and took over. The good news was that since I owned and well cared for the attached lot and paid a yearly additional hefty real estate tax because of it, I could simply have a fence put up and totally enclose and incorporate my additional lot with the rest of my property, and thereby have a yard for the dog, the boys, and me to run free and play without fear of the dog getting out and roaming the neighborhood or getting hit by a car.

The fence company came out to survey the land and got all of the appropriate zoning licenses necessary to put the fence up and completely enclose my property. The day after the first posts were cemented into the ground, the same neighbors who had never spoken to and spurned our family, who had never returned a wave or even a smile, who had enjoyed using not just the our attached lot, but even our front lawn property, came knocking on my door demanding to know just what I was building because it looked like prison.

I went on to tell them that I was simply putting up a fence as we had purchased a German shepherd dog, who would be massive when full grown. I did not want him roaming the neighborhood, and we wanted a safe place to play and allow him to exercise. They asked if I had the proper permits to do so and I thanked them and assured them that I did. Apparently after they left, they called the folks in charge of zoning because I received a visit from the zoning commissioner a short time later. He came into my house, took one look at my dog and saw why I needed the fence. I asked if there was anything out of order with the permits and he assured me that they were in order.

I asked why he was here and he said that my neighbors did not want me to fence in my property. He went on to say that it was within my legal right to fence in my property, but since my neighbors did so much for our city, he was going to have to change the zoning permit unless I would consider either not putting the fence up at all or move it back away from the property division line leaving some of my property outside of the fenced in area. I asked if he would like to take this up with my lawyer to which he said he would rather not and he left again saying he would just revoke the permit.

I saw my neighbors out walking through my lot and looking around so I went out to talk with them and show them our big dog in hopes that they would understand that the purpose for the fence was also to keep him safe and perhaps even to give our neighbors peace of mind knowing he was safely enclosed in his own yard. When I asked just what their objection to my fence was they said that by me enclosing my property, they would no longer be able to enjoy the beautiful scenery of my property. They enjoyed looking out at the pretty trees, nice shrubbery, and all of the nature filled wonders that had been created on my property. They were musicians and as they practiced early in the mornings they would enjoy the sun rising over my property. They said that the fence posts which now were already deeply cemented into the ground, were also ugly and would take away the ambiance of the neighborhood.

I must confess, I was very angry that they were making this so difficult for me to use my own land. Additionally, this was during the time of my highly contested divorce/child custody case so tensions were already at full capacity. Nevertheless, I cast my burdens before the Lord and went into deep prayer. People whom I talked to about the fence said that I should tell my neighbors to go away. Really they said go somewhere else, but I knew that was not of the Lord. After praying, I decided to move my fence back away from the property line by five feet and felt this was a compromise I could live with, even though I would not be getting the full benefit of all of my land.

Upon telling my neighbors what I thought they would receive as great news, they quickly rebutted and said they would rather I move my fence back by ten feet. They had the nerve to say that what I offered as a compromise was not good enough for them. I again went before the Lord and told him that I had done my part and now I was going to have to just put the fence where I initially had planned since they were not appreciative of my new offer. In the meantime, the fence company told me that they would have to charge me to remove the deeply cemented posts if I wanted them moved back and wondered who in the world would ever consider doing that. They advised me that they had the correct permits and I had a right to put the fence right where it was already started. It seemed like the matter was settled.

But God interceded as I was seeking a word from him through reading and studying my Bible. "Just because something is technically legal does not mean that it is spiritually appropriate. If I went around doing whatever I thought I could get by with, I would be a slave to my whims" (1 Corinthians 6:12 MSG). It became very clear to me what I was supposed to do—share the gospel of Jesus' love with them.

I wrote a long letter to my neighbors and apologized that if I had ever done anything, for any reason, that may have driven them to ignore us or feel that they could not speak to us, I was begging their forgiveness. If I had offended them in any way, I begged their forgiveness. I went on to write that our Lord Jesus in the Bible teaches us to love our neighbors, and I had fallen short and for this I begged their forgiveness. This land did not belong to me, it was my Lord and Savior Jesus the Christ's land, and I was but a steward caring for the land.

Then I reminded them that I was well within my legal rights to put the fence where I had initially decided, but Paul, the Jewish apostle wrote in 1 Corinthians 6:12 that just because something is legally right, does not always make it the correct thing to do in all cases. Therefore, I was going to immediately pay to have the already cemented posts removed and placed not five feet, but ten feet away from the property line just as they requested. Additionally, the ten feet of land that was now annexed to their property, could be used by them for whatever purposes they desired and they could even hang any decorative items they wanted to on the fence to make it more attractive to them. I made it very clear that the only reason I was joyfully doing this was because of what Jesus Christ did for me (and them) on the cross two thousand years ago. This was the perfect opportunity to show love and share Christ Jesus with my neighbors and start a dialogue that has led to us being great neighbors.

I am still praying that this love shown to them will eventually help lead them to accept Jesus as their Lord. I believe the Lord set it up from the beginning. Some have asked me how I held my peace as my neighbors went from five feet not being good enough to asking for ten additional feet. The answer is simple, nothing but the Lord and staying in his living word. It was and remains my hope and prayer, that I can model the love and mercy of our God.

Fruit of the Spirit: Faithfulness

We turn now to our next aspect of the Fruit of the Spirit, faithfulness. This signifies a Christian's trust in Jesus Christ to provide salvation.[36] Faith deals with intellectual belief and relational trust. In the Bible, faith as belief and trust encapsulates believing first that Jesus is Lord, and trusting that God the Father, God the Son, and God the Holy Spirit are reliable, and able to do, what they say they will do, very notably, provide salvation. [37]

1 Corinthians 10:13 reminds us, "God is faithful, who will not suffer you to be tempted above that ye are able." 2 Thessalonians 3:3 states, "The Lord is faithful, who shall establish you, and keep you from evil." Our God is faithful so we can rest assured that what he has said, he will do. We can stand on his promises without wavering, and we too can be faithful. Jinkins notes that the Holy Spirit gifts us with a "faith-sight" which enables us to see who we are in Christ. The Spirit acts to make us one with Christ so that his life becomes our own and then we in turn are endowed with extraordinary insight.[38] With this "faith-sight" we can have the ability to believe that we truly can do all things through Christ because he is the one really doing them. Our faith rests on his sovereign ability, not our limited human ability.

With a faith grounded in God's ability to do even the impossible, how can we fail at reaching the world for Christ? Whom shall we fear?

---

[36] Longenecker, *Galatians*, 262.

[37] Grenz, *Pocket Dictionary*, 50.

[38] Jinkins, *Invitation*, 205-206.

What land shall we not go to and make disciples? The problem comes when we have *oligopistia* or "little faith" like the disciples in Matthew 17:20. The disciples' little faith was really incomplete, wavering faith, which amounted really to no faith and thus, they were unable to cast out the demon from the afflicted boy.[39] The Holy Spirit has given us the ability to have the faith we need to do all that God has asked of us. He would not ask us to do anything that he has not equipped us to do, so let us faithfully fulfill his disciple-making commission.

> *When they came to the crowd, a man came to him, knelt before him, and said, "Lord, have mercy on my son, for he is an epileptic and he suffers terribly; he often falls into the fire and often into the water. And I brought him to your disciples, but they could not cure him." Jesus answered, "you faithless and perverse generation, how much longer must I be with you? How much longer must I put up with you? Bring him here to me." And Jesus rebuked the demon, and it came out of him, and the boy was cured instantly. Then the disciples came to Jesus privately and said, "Why could we not cast it*

---

[39] S.C. Barton, "Faith" in *Dictionary of Jesus and the Gospels*, ed., Andrew T. Le Peu (Downers Grove: InterVarsity, 1992), 224.

out?" He said to them, "Because of your little faith. For truly I tell you, if you have faith the size of a mustard seed, you will say to this mountain, 'move from here to there,' and it will move; and nothing will be impossible for you." (Matthew 17:14-20 NRSV)

In Matthew 17:14 Jesus, Peter, James, and John are just coming down from the mountain where Jesus was transfigured. France summarizes the scene, "From the mountains of revelation Jesus and the three disciples come down to a scene of demonic oppression and human weakness which evokes a remarkably strong emotional response from Jesus (v. 17). The parallel with Moses' experience at Sinai is suggestive: he came down from the mountain with the tablets of God's revelation and was faced by a scene of religious apostasy which caused him to break the tablets in his anger."[40]

---

[40] France, *The Gospel of Matthew,* 657. This is a strong OT allusion, as the sinful children of Israel, having been freed from bondage in Egypt, having seen the Red Sea parted before their very eyes, and having seen and benefited from countless miracles, have so soon forgotten, the "Lord their God, who brought them out of Egypt," when Moses (now returning from the mountaintop experience with God) was absent. No leader, no power. Now, Jesus having been absent from the people and some of His disciples, returns from the mountain of Transfiguration, to be confronted by a crowd having witnessed a failure by his disciples to perform as authorized. No leader, no power.

Verse 14 continues, "A man came to him, knelt before him." Hagner concludes that in using the Greek words for "came to" and "kneeling down," Matthew is presenting the man as worshiping Jesus.[41] Crowds seem to follow Jesus wherever he or his disciples are, and this occasion was no exception. The man coming forward out of a crowd is reminiscent of other crowd scenes (Matthew 8:1, 9:36, 14:14, 15:30, and 19:2), where there were people in need of Jesus' help. Matthew's use of the Greek terms for "approaches" and "kneels," are commonly used when he is describing the supplications to Jesus by people who are either themselves sick or are seeking help for someone else.[42] Whether this represents worshiping Jesus as deity, or simply respecting his authority and asking for help in a most reverent manner, it was clear to the petitioners that Jesus alone (and those he authorized) could uniquely heal.

The father's request of the Lord in verse fifteen brings to mind other prayerful requests such as the Canaanite woman in Matthew 15:22 shouting, "Have mercy on me, Lord, son of David." Then in 15:25, she came and knelt before Jesus saying, "Lord, help me." The powerful image of kneeling before the Lord is often matched with the messianic

---

[41] Donald A. Hagner, *Matthew 14-28*, vol. 33B Word Biblical Commentary (Nashville: Thomas Nelson, 1995), 503. First, recognizing that Jesus was the One to "come to" for help and then "kneeling" before Jesus, Hagner believes this to be a sign of reverent respect.

[42] Donald Senior, *Matthew*, Abingdon New Testament Commentaries (Nashville: Abingdon Press, 1998), 199.

title of "son of David." This recognizes the authority and the majesty due a king. In fact, Gundry argues that the words that Matthew used in verse fifteen to state the man's request, in its original language, served to emphasize Jesus' deity. Gundry goes on to state outright: "The man's first words constitute a Christological confession and plea, then, rather than a historically descriptive statement."[43]

In verse sixteen, the man now tells Jesus that he had taken his son to the disciples, but they could not cure him. Is it possible that the inability of Jesus' disciples to heal could cause perhaps even other believers to doubt Jesus' power? After all, it was Jesus who had given them the authority to exorcise in Matthew 10:1 and 8. The man probably had come looking for Jesus in the beginning having heard that he could exorcise demons, however not finding Jesus, his hopes had rested upon Jesus' disciples, who utterly failed.

The immediate question that comes to mind is who is Jesus rebuking? Is he rebuking the man who brought the request? Is he rebuking the disciples? Is he rebuking the crowd? Or is he rebuking a combination of people? France concludes that this outburst by Jesus is directed toward the whole generation, and certainly not at the man

---

[43] Robert H. Gundry, *Matthew: A Commentary on His Literary and Theological Art* (Grand Rapids, Michigan: Eerdmans, 1982), 349. The man, by asking for mercy, is recognizing that Jesus is not just another man, but as a Christological confession, he perhaps is recognizing Jesus to be The Christ, the long awaited Messiah.

who seemed to believe in Jesus' power, but perhaps not in the disciple's power.[44]

France explains, "If even the disciples from their position of special privilege (Matthew 13:11-17), do not have the faith to draw God's saving power, what hope is there for the entire generation?" Therefore, Matthew's insertion of "and perverse" only serves to further highlight the corruption of unbelieving Israel.[45]

Jesus' frustration is evident by this question and Bauer notes Jesus is really again alluding to his coming death, and the fact that he will not be there much longer.[46] Perhaps having just come down from the

---

[44] France, *The Gospel of Matthew, 660*. In Matthew, the man knew to go directly to Jesus once he saw Jesus approach the crowd. He must have known Jesus to be a merciful healer, as he asked Jesus to have mercy on his son, but never directly asks Jesus for specific help. For Matthew, Jesus would help by healing, but healing was not his focus. Faith, as will be seen later was to be the focus. In Mark 9:22 however, the father says, "…but if you are able to do anything, have pity on us and help us." Mark is highlighting the desperateness of the father, and building the action for a culminating miracle of exorcism as the climax of the Mark passage and as the main theme of Jesus healing.

[45] France, *The Gospel of Matthew*, 661.

[46] David R. Bauer, *The Structure of Matthew's Gospel: A Study in Literary Design*, Journal for the Study of the New Testament Supplement Series, 31 (Sheffield: Almond Press, 1988),98. Interestingly, there is agreement among Matthew, Mark and Luke, that Jesus asked this question. Each of the Synoptic Evangelists were compelled to include this question. The nearer context of each of the three Synoptic pericopes, included a passion prediction both prior to and immediatley following, signifying the impending death of Jesus, who would soon be gone, leaving the disciples alone to carry out His mission. Additionally, this pericope, in all three of the Synoptics, is a part of a larger segment which includes the Disciples' and Jesus' journey from Galilee to Jerusalem, where Jesus would suffer and die on the cross.

mountaintop experience in which he encountered Moses, Jesus was exasperated by the breakdown of power in the kingdom, in his absence as evidenced by the disciples' inability to heal. The hardheartedness of the crowd seems to be the concern for Jesus as he asks how much longer he must put up with them.[47]

Matthew omits Mark's lengthy story of the conversation between Jesus and the father regarding the history of the possession and the father's belief or lack thereof. Now without any hesitation, Jesus takes it upon himself to silence the demon tormenting the boy and cures him. In Luke and Matthew's version, there is no long drawn out exorcism, rather, the boy was cured instantly upon Jesus' rebuke.

Once the disciples were alone with Jesus, they asked why they could not cast out the demon. It was not unusual for the disciples to ask for an explanation after a notable incident or saying by Jesus (for example in Matthew 13:10, 19:10, 24:3). Jesus responds that they could not cast out the demon, "because of your little faith." Matthew goes into what he deems as the main lesson of the story, namely, faith in God to do anything. This is not Jesus' first time charging the disciples

---

[47] Daniel Patte, *The Gospel According to Matthew: A Structural Commentary on Matthew's Faith* (Philadelphia: Fortress, 1987), 240. Patte notes that Matthew 16:14-16 and 17:4, reveal that the people who observe Jesus from afar, believe him to be one of the prophets, like John the Baptist, Elijah, Jeremiah, or another of the prophets of old. They clearly have not recognized Jesus as the Christ, the Son of God, although they may recognize him as someone sent from God.

with "little faith" (6:30, 8:26, 14:31 and 16:18), but now, the results could have had serious repercussions for this young boy.[48] Luz remarks, "Matthew found it in the sayings source (q 12:28) and employed it several times in his gospel. Little faith is the faith of those who set out with Jesus only to lose heart. Little faith is faith mingled with fear and doubt. Little faith is the faith of those who would like to believe but cannot. For Matthew, little faith also means doubting ones' authority to work miracles."[49]

Faith that acknowledges God's power is available to do the impossible. The impossible is represented by moving mountains just by speaking it so. This is clearly a hyperbolic analogy that drives home the point that with God, nothing shall be impossible.[50] In order for God to act on behalf of his followers, and do what is impossible for

---

[48] France, *The Gospel of Matthew,* 662; Ironically, in Senior's, *Matthew,* 200, he remarks that even though the disciples are first-hand participants of Jesus' teachings of discipleship, their yet weak faith, will lead to even other failures as they journey to Jerusalem. Ultimately Peter will even deny Christ.

[49] Ulrich Luz, *The Theology of the Gospel of Matthew,* New Testament Theology (New York: Cambridge University Publishing, 1995), 68-69. Although found in Q, Luke does not use the saying in this parallel story.

[50] Hagner, *Matthew 14-28,* 505; France, *Gospel of Matthew,* 662; and Patte, *Gospel According to Matthew,* 240 , all have similar conclusions namely that while faith enables, the lack of faith prevents the desired action. Davies and Allison in *Matthew 8-18,* 728-729, go on to note that faith is the currency required by God, for Him to act on behalf of man. Faith is never a power in and of itself, but instead, faith, expressed as trust in our God through Jesus, calls upon God to perform His mighty deeds.

man, he requires but mustard seed-sized genuine faith that is deeply and permanently embedded in the heart, rather than wavering mountain-sized cheap faith, which is in word only and blows away at the first hint of any winds of adversity or uncertainty. (See Appendix 2 for an application of Matthew 17:14-20 faith.)

When we begin to consistently walk in and not just speak of the unwavering faith that only our covenant-keeping, Christ-resurrecting God could stir in our hearts, then we can and will accomplish all that the Lord has set before us to do. Nothing shall be impossible for this mountain-moving people of God, who speak by faith, then walk by faith, acting as if they cannot fail. "These things and greater" spoken of by Jesus, we shall do because of our faith in the omnipotent God and Father of our Lord Jesus Christ. So while it is impossible to please God without faith, faith is not the end of our walk, but really a beginning and basis of our walk with God.

> *But also for this very reason, giving all diligence, add to your faith virtue, to virtue knowledge, to knowledge self-control, to self-control perseverance, to perseverance godliness, to godliness brotherly kindness, and to brotherly kindness love. For if these things are yours*

and abound, you will be neither barren nor unfruitful in the knowledge of our Lord Jesus Christ. For he who lacks these things is shortsighted, even to blindness, and has forgotten that he was cleansed from his old sins. Therefore, brethren, be even

more diligent to make your call and election sure, for if you do these things you will never stumble; for so an entrance will be supplied to you abundantly into the everlasting kingdom of our Lord and savior Jesus Christ. (2 Peter 1:5-11)

How blessed it is to walk by faith through difficult and trying times of affliction and still honor God. We can do this because of the hope that we have in Jesus Christ.

We also glory in tribulations, knowing that tribulation produces perseverance; and perseverance, character; and character, hope. Now hope does not disappoint, because the love of God has been poured out in our hearts by the Holy Spirit who was given to us. (Romans 5:3-5)

Fruit of the Spirit: Self-Control

The final aspect of the Fruit of the Spirit is self-control. Longenecker notes that "self-control" was an important virtue during the Hellenistic times of Paul and could be contrasted against the drunken, carousing works of the flesh seen in 5:19-21. Even Socrates and Plato wrote of self-control as an ethical term. References to self-control (as a noun) occur two other times in the New Testament (Acts 24:25 and 2 Peter 1:6).[51] Other translations may use the word temperance, but the central theme regards guarding against over-indulgence and unrestrained improper behavior. DeSilva asserts that even in the apocryphal text of 4 Macc. 1:30-31, there is further confirmation that this self-control is a matter of mastering one's fleshly human passions. In fact, it may be seen as the foundational "fruit" owing to the fact that the passions of the flesh are the main hindrance to every virtue.[52]

The world is intently watching, and unfortunately waiting, for those who would claim to be Christ-believers to make a wrong step and fall into sin. This, in the world's mind, would be a chance to expose the hypocrisy of the people of God. "These Christians say one thing on Sunday, but do another thing throughout the week," they say. "Why would I want to become a Christian, when these self-proclaimed

---

[51] Longenecker, *Galatians*, 263.

[52] DeSilva, *New Testament*, 521.

believers are involved in the same behaviors that I am immersed in," they say. What the world does not realize is that Christ died for our sins—past, present, and future. Even though we are Christians, "All have sinned and fall short of God's glory." However, the God of love, peace, and faithfulness reminds us through his Holy Spirit, that "if we confess our sins, he being just and again faithful, will forgive us of our sins and cleanse us" with Christ's shed blood (1John 1:9).

However, if we as the children of God are to take the call to world discipleship seriously, we have got to depend on, submit to, and continuously pray for, not just the mere indwelling, but for the over-flowing power of the Holy Spirit. In doing so, he can exercise in us, not only self-control and obedience, but also manifest the complete Fruit of the Spirit for the world to see, marvel at, and ultimately desire.

Paul says it well in Galatians 5:24-25, "Now those who belong to Christ Jesus have crucified the flesh with its passions and desires. If we live by the spirit, let us also walk by the spirit." It is time for all Christians everywhere and in every stratum of life, Jew and Greek, black and white, slave and free, male and female, rich and poor to not just talk the talk, but walk the walk of the way, the truth and the life. For there is no other way to the Father, so we must first share with the world the love and the fruit of our God's presence in our lives.

Action Steps

Have you been disappointed by people who have said that they would always be right by your side, but have abandoned you?

Have you lost your sense of any hope in this life and find yourself with little or no joy?

Do you feel aimless and have a lack of direction or purpose for your life?

Do you find yourself ever asking just why you are even here on this earth?

Do you want to experience the hope that comes from an all-powerful God who is trustworthy and faithful and who promises to never leave you on your own?

You can begin living life to its fullest, experiencing the richness of all God has to offer, and knowing that God wants the absolute best for you. Just say out loud right now:

Lord Jesus, you are the only one I can trust to help me and save me. I have not been a trustworthy person and have hurt others with my lack of honesty. I have selfishly put my concerns ahead of everyone else's for too long and I am sorry for all of my wrong doing against others and you. Lord Jesus, I receive the hope that you offer by my acceptance of your death on the cross to pay the penalty for all of my wrong doings. I want to have the faith that pleases you, Lord Jesus, so I ask you to be the sole director of my life and invite you to live in my heart as my Savior. In Jesus name I pray. Amen.

BORA BORA, TAHITI. MAY 2014

Chapter 11
"I" Is for Inspire and Intercede

Who comforts us in all our tribulation that we may be able to comfort those who are in any trouble, with the comfort with which we ourselves are comforted by God.
(2 Corinthians 1:4)

Let us begin this chapter on inspiring, encouraging, and interceding for others by examining 2 Corinthians 1:3-4 from three translations.

"Blessed *be* the God and father of our Lord Jesus Christ, the father of mercies and God of all comfort, **who comforts us in all our tribulation, that we may be able to comfort those who are in any trouble**, with the comfort with which we ourselves are comforted by God" (emphasis added).

"Blessed be the God and father of our Lord Jesus Christ, the father of sympathy (pity and mercy) and the God [who is the source] of every comfort (consolation and encouragement), **who comforts (consoles and encourages) us in every trouble (calamity and affliction), so that we may also be able to comfort (console and encourage) those who are in any kind of trouble *or* distress**, with the comfort (consolation and encouragement) with which we ourselves are comforted (consoled and encouraged) by God" (AMP emphasis added).

"All praise to the God and father of our master, Jesus the Messiah. Father of all mercy. God of all healing counsel. **He comes alongside us when we go through hard times, and before you know it, he brings us alongside someone else who is going through hard times so that we can be there for that person** just as God was there for us. We have plenty of hard times that come from following the messiah, but no more so than the good times of his healing comfort—we get a full measure of that, too" (2 Corinthians 1:3-5 MSG emphasis added).

It should be clear from this reading in 2 Corinthians, that the sovereign God of the universe not only gives us clear admonition, but expects us to inspire, encourage and intercede for others going through any adversity. Note that as we are all going through one trial or another at any given time, we should not wait until we are free and clear of any problems before helping others. Otherwise, we might never take the opportunity to help others, as we are busy constantly wallowing in our own pain.

However, it is vitally important that we understand we cannot and are not to intercede for others in our own power and strength. God never asks us to work in our own power because alone we do not have any power. We are to depend on him and use what he gives us to help others. We were not made to live this life independently, but instead we were made to depend on God, who quite frankly often uses others to help us. Interestingly, the people God chooses to help us are often not our first choice, if a choice at all. We must remain prayerfully open to whoever or whatever God uses to speak to us. God may not speak to us through a burning bush as he did Moses, or he may not send the angel Gabriel to bring you great tidings of joy directly from God's throne room, but rest assured he does and will speak to his children. The question is will you be listening, and then will you obey?

We cannot escape James 5:16, reminding us to confess our faults to someone who can then pray for us. Yes, we can and should pray for ourselves, but many times we also need one another. It is critically important to have faithful, godly, trustworthy friends, who knowing God's truth, hearing God's truth, and living God's truth can speak truth to us even when we do not want to hear it. More importantly, we need those who will intercede for us through prayer.

Take the time to pray right now to our Lord Jesus about who those people are in your life that you can confess your faults to and who will lovingly pray for you and hold you accountable without passing condemnation upon you.

So, You Are Having a Bad Day?
Cancer, Cancer, Cancer...

Just as we will all need some encouragement at some point in our lives, we must take every opportunity to inspire and intercede for others going through adversity even when we may feel that we are the ones in need of encouragement at the time. God honors us as we put aside our own present concerns to bless others. When I make a conscious decision to be a blessing to others who are hurting, what I thought was a major disruption in my life suddenly pales in comparison to the issues of others.

I am reminded of a fine summer Wednesday in 2005. It was not really a fine day in my mind at the time. In fact, it was a time filled with extreme turbulence that I felt neither I nor my sons deserved and certainly would have never volunteered for. Truth be told, up until that point, I felt that it was one of the worse days in life. I later came to find out that day was just the beginning of sorrows that God would use for my good to help begin to mold me into the image of his son and our Savior, Jesus, so that I could bless someone else at the appointed time.

Nevertheless, as I arrived at my office building two hours late, I was feeling quite sorry for myself. I walked onto the elevator only to be immediately engaged by an older women sobbing uncontrollably. As we were the only ones on the elevator, it was rather difficult to ignore her and quite frankly, I had decided long ago that instead of ignoring people and acting as if they are not there, to always speak the love of Christ in an "elevator ministry" of sorts. I asked her what was wrong, and she did not hesitate to tell me that she had just come from one doctor's office and was going to another having just found out that she had throat cancer. The Lord immediately impressed on me right there in the elevator to ask her if I could pray for her.

Most people in a dire circumstance, no matter what they believe or do not believe, will never turn down a prayer at that moment. I am sure you have heard that there are no atheists on planes that are crashing to the ground. It is moments like these that many people will be open to our loving God who has been patiently waiting for them to surrender to him. She gladly accepted my offer to pray and I am sure that that elevator never heard a cry to God as it did in those few seconds. I must admit, it seemed like time stopped, and that I was able to pray just what was needed. As I said amen, the elevator doors opened, she thanked me, hugged me and very confidently walked out of that elevator. I never saw her again, but I cannot help but believe that our God used pathetic me to intercede on her behalf that "fine" day.

When I reached my floor and walked into my office, I had three patients waiting for me in three different treatment rooms. I have a wonderful staff (Right Hand Tenda Linda, Lovely Luba, Sister Kathy, and Walk with the King Amanda) who assessed the situation and then directed me into treatment room #3 first only to find a middle-aged lady crying. Now while I realize that no one really wants a root canal, there was really no need for her to be crying already. When I asked her what was wrong, she told me that she had just found out her younger brother, only twenty years old, had been diagnosed with cancer. Incredible, I had just gotten of the elevator with a lady with cancer and now my first patient tells me that her baby brother has cancer. I immediately asked her if I could pray with her and she accepted.

The Lord has put it on my heart to ask to pray with each of my patients. Many times, sensing fear from the patients, I have just grabbed their hands and prayed without asking. This day we cried, prayed, and then agreed to trust in the Lord to do what he knows how best to do.

As I went in to see my next patient waiting in treatment room #2, she was an elderly lady who told me that she was not sure if she was up to receiving any treatment that day. She had just found out that her husband of several decades was besieged with cancer. Immediately, I went into prayer for her husband and their family without bothering to ask if I could pray. I prayed at a feverish rate for quite a while as I knew that there was something more operating on this "fine" day.

I dismissed the patient and went into my private office weeping uncontrollably asking God to intercede on behalf of these three people in a row who either had cancer themselves or a loved-one stricken with one of the most fear provoking diseases. It was at that moment that I distinctly remember hearing the voice of God say to me, "So you are having a bad day? Which one of these people would you rather trade places with?" I asked the Lord to forgive me for complaining about my little petty issues and for my "woe is me attitude" when I serve a God who can do anything but fail. I asked the Lord to help me to take my focus off of me, myself, and I and to help me to trust him to care for me, while I did my best to allow him to use me as he saw fit to **inspire** and **intercede** for others going through the storms of life.

To be blessed, be a blessing to others, who can then bless others and be blessed...

As I give precedence to interceding, encouraging and caring for others, God has often begun to reveal the resolutions to my own issues. He was already working on them, but I was too blind to see it worrying about the problem instead of trusting him to fix it. When I put my efforts into encouraging and praying for others, it is as if God looks down and says, "Now that is what I am talking about, my son. While you are blessing others, I will take care of you. That is part of my plan for all people. Be a blessing to others, just as I have blessed you, and then I will bless you even more so you can be a blessing to others who can bless others as they have been blessed."

God's economy and God's math is unlike man's limited thinking. Just when we think we have reached the pinnacle of what our loving God can or will do for us, our great provider breaks through our self-imposed glass ceiling to remind us that when he says that "nothing is impossible" for him, he means just that. He may choose to express his love for us in a variety of endless and inexhaustible ways. This may include his peace fulfilling gift of real life tangible solutions to whatever may be plaguing our lives or deteriorating our walk of faith.

We are to comfort others with the same comfort that God has given us. Whatever comfort or relief we received, we should give to those who are hurting. Who among us can say that they have not faced some hardship at some point in their lives? Having gone through a valley experience ourselves, and in order to help fulfill the God-given mission of comfort for some other, we can ask ourselves:

What might have brought more comfort during my trying times?
What might I have hoped to have received in the midnight hour?
What helped keep hope alive and well during my own dry desert season?
What did God do through another person that brought great relief?
What words of comfort brought a whisper of peace to my ears?

Once you have answered these questions, do not hesitate to do them for others going through a storm and even go beyond what was done or what we wished would have been done for us. Like our God who gives abundantly more than we ask or think, we should strive to do more than enough. One possible goal of this Corinthian mandate is to allow God to use us to help minimize the pain and suffering of others especially knowing what the pain and suffering felt like when we were on the receiving end.

There may be consequences that result in suffering for our sinful behavior, but I cannot escape the fact that God being full of grace and mercy certainly expects his people to exercise grace and mercy.

We Serve Jesus When We Serve Others

When we take our minds off of our own personal adversities and concentrate on helping others, we are truly serving Jesus. This obedient service to God in spite of our own suffering often results in God moving and responding to our painful circumstances. What a mighty and generous God we serve.

The enemy of our souls, knowing the power of prayer, would have us not pray. In fact, Satan knows that if he can pile enough worries, pain, fear, and disappointment on our heads, we might feel so helpless that we do not even want to pray. It is despondent times like these that despite how we feel, we must press through and we must pray and call out to God for help. It is times like this when we may need to **intercede** for someone and pray for them. It is important to note that the enemy will do all he can to lie to us and have us wrongly believe that our problems are so unsolvable that there is no need to pray for ourselves. Hear our God and what he promises in 2 Chronicles 7:14.

If my people who are called by my name will humble themselves, and pray and seek my face, and turn from their wicked ways, then I will hear from heaven, and will forgive their sin and heal their land.

This is a conditional clause that starts with what God expects of us and ends with what he will do for us. Here is my pneumonic acronym to help me remember this scripture: "We **help st**op and he **h**ears-for-**h**ealing."

Our job is to be **humble** and confess that we need God's help, **pray** to God asking for his help, **seek** God's help only, and **turn** away as best as we can from any known sin in our lives as we focus on him for our help. When we do this, first God **hears** our prayers and will **forgive** our sins in response to our contritely asking and turning away from sin. God will then **heal** and provide for our needs.

Prayer is a wonderful gift that God has given us to use, not only during a storm in our lives, but each and every day at all times. More importantly, we must **inspire, encourage, and intercede** for others in prayer as they are struggling with the cares of this life even when we are in the midst of our own trial. God expects us to comfort others and he will bless us for comforting others. The good news is that although we may not be able to do this in our own strength, he will provide the strength for us to accomplish it for his glory alone.

Action Steps

Is there something you are struggling with today?

Do you feel as if you need someone to inspire, encourage or intercede in prayer for you?

Is there someone you know who needs help, but you just cannot muster up the strength to help them?

Perhaps you do not know how to help them because you are in your own raging battle that you feel you are losing.

There is an answer to your problem. There is a God who is able to do more than you could ever imagine and who has been patiently waiting for you to simply ask for his help. His name is Jesus.

Cry out wherever you are right now and say:

Jesus, I need your help. Jesus, you have already interceded for me by dying on the cross and paying the price for my sins. This day, I humble myself, seek you, and turn away from the sins I have been committing. I accept your intercession on the cross and receive you as my Savior and Lord. Thank you for hearing my prayer, forgiving my sins, and healing my wounds. In Jesus name I pray. Amen.

If you just prayed this prayer, then be prepared for a whole different way of living this life. You can now call on Jesus Christ, your intercessor, to help you with any problem and to give you the strength and knowledge to help **inspire, encourage, and intercede** for others, even when you may find yourself challenged by the affairs of this fallen world.

IT'S PROOF TIME...

Bora Bora, May 2014

CHAPTER 12
"M" IS FOR MEDITATE ON GOD'S SPECIFIC WORD

*Finally, brethren, whatever things are true, whatever things are noble, whatever things are just, whatever things are pure, whatever things are lovely, whatever things are of good report, if there is any virtue and if there is anything praiseworthy—**meditate** on these things. The things which you learned and received and heard and saw in me, these do, and the God of peace will be with you.* (Philippians 4:8-9 emphasis added)

Recognizing that our minds are a battle ground that Satan would love to dominate and control, 2 Corinthians 10:5 gives us clear instruction to "bring every thought into captivity to the obedience of Christ." We should not allow our minds to even speculate about the possibility of doing evil, but when that evil thought comes into our minds say immediately, "In the name of Jesus, I take you captive and expel you back to the pit of hell from whence you came." I cannot allow sinful thoughts to marinate in my mind. Why? *Because I am weak all by myself.* I cannot wage and win any war on my own in my own strength, doing things my way and not God's way.

God, knowing us better than we know ourselves, does not want us to dwell on sinful evil thoughts so that we can rationalize why we should not follow through with the sin in question. Often times, the more we even consider or worse yet "fantasize" about sinful thoughts, the less evil it appears to be. In fact, we may begin to compromise and tell ourselves that we deserve a little fun once in a while. After all, no one will ever find out and even if they do, we are surely not the first or only one doing this thing. Dear friend, this is a slippery slope trick of the devil that leads to nowhere good. God, understanding our gullibility and having full knowledge of the utter hatred that Satan has especially for those who would desire to be obedient to God's word, commands his children to have no part of those evil thoughts. He knows that sinful thoughts may lead to sinful actions.

That is one of the reasons he is specific about what we should **meditate** on. Things that are true, noble, just, pure, lovely, of good report, praiseworthy, and virtuous. God knows that when we dwell on the "negative" aspects of so many things, this often leads to a bitter, complaining spirit that is not pleasing to God and is really sin.

Meditate on God's Specific Word for Your Circumstance

What is always true, noble, just, pure, lovely, of good report, praiseworthy, and virtuous? The word of God. What shall one do with the word of God? The Psalmist answers in 119:11, "Your word I have hidden in my heart that I might not sin against you." In order to help keep my heart from sin, I must hide God's word in my heart. This means I must read daily and continuously, God's word. I must **meditate** on what God's word means in light of the circumstances that I may face. I must memorize God's word so that it is deeply embedded and a part of my very being. Then when there is confrontation with the enemy that is sure to come and I am squeezed by the vice grip of life's troubles, the word of God will come pouring forth from me like rivers of God's righteousness. This is the goal and my prayer.

I must confess that this does not always happen, therefore, I must be submitted and surrendered to the Holy Spirit and do all that I can to bury God's word in my heart. For me that means writing specific scriptures, truths, and promises of God relative to the adversity, trial, or concern at hand on index cards and carry them with me. God's word has an answer to every question in my life. I just have to do the leg work and study to find the answer. Fortunately, internet sites like Bible Gateway and concordances in the back of most Bibles, make searching for a scripture about a certain topic easier. This search always starts with prayer and asking God to give me the wisdom I lack to find his answer to the question at hand. As I go through my day, I pull out the index cards and read, meditate, memorize, and seek to apply these scriptures to my current life situations.

As I memorize the scriptures, I have less need to carry them with me, but there are times when I will keep key scripture index cards handy in my top pocket to pull out and beat the devil back. Ephesians 6:17 says the word of God is the sword of the Spirit. It is a weapon that God has provided for us to fight against any spiritual wickedness. Why would we leave these weapon tucked away on the shelf?

During certain periods of my life, it has been crucial for me to **meditate** on God's specific word for the trial I was facing. A few years back, I was in Park City, Utah with my two sons. We were enjoying horseback riding, hiking, and fishing during a summer conference. My ex-wife, knowing I was out of the state, came with some of her associates, illegally entered my home, and removed a number of items without my permission. This happened a second time when she knew I was away from my home. I felt very violated and defenseless as the authorities would do nothing about this situation.

While doing my morning devotional reading, I heard a truck coming down the street, fear struck my heart that a truck would pull up to my home and clean me out for good. As I watched the truck pass by my home, I suddenly realized this paranoid fear was nothing but the enemy attempting to disrupt my life. There was absolutely no reason why anyone would legitimately come and remove anything from my home. I owed no one, I had promised no one anything that I had not delivered on, and there was no legal reason my ex-wife or anyone else should ever come into my home without my permission. My conscious was completely clear.

I cried out loud, "Lord, help me, there is absolutely no reason for me to have this fear, help me." Just then I looked down at the notebook I use to jot down any thoughts, revelations, or insights that may come to me as I am studying God's word. There on the left hand column of a page was a scripture that one of my brothers had given me to look up the week before regarding fear. I immediately looked it up and about fell over when I read the scripture.

> ***Fear not, for I am with you;*** *be not dismayed, for I am your God. I will strengthen you,* ***yes, I will help you****, I will uphold you with my righteous right hand. Behold, all those who were incensed against you shall be ashamed and disgraced; they shall be as nothing, and those who strive with you shall perish. You shall seek them and not find them—those who contended with you. Those who war against you shall be as nothing, as a nonexistent thing. For I, the* LORD *your God, will hold your right hand, saying to you,* ***"Fear not, I will help you."*** (Isaiah 41:10-13 emphasis added)

The God of the universe, who has all power in his hands, gave me a definite answer. I immediately felt a peace that could have only come from God Almighty. I fell down on my face and began to ask God for forgiveness for not trusting in him fully. I immediately wrote that scripture on an index card. To this very day, if any fear starts to creep into my life, I pull that same tattered yellow index card out and begin to recite God's word as he speaks directly to me. I began to look up other scriptures reminding me to fear not, and wrote those out on index cards to carry with me as well.

> *You will **not** need to fight in this battle. Position yourselves, stand still and see the salvation of the Lord, who is with you, O Judah and Jerusalem. Do **not fear** or be dismayed; tomorrow go out against them, for the Lord is with you.* (2 Chronicles 20:17 emphasis added)

> *Though an army may encamp against me, my heart shall **not fear**; though war may rise against me, in this I will be confident.* (Psalm 27:3 emphasis added)

> *In God (I will praise his word), in God I have put my trust; I will **not fear**. What can flesh do to me?* (Psalm 56:4 emphasis added)

> ***Fear not**, for I have redeemed you; I have called you by your name; you are mine.* (Isaiah 43:1 emphasis added)

*For God has **not** given us a spirit of **fear**, but of power and of love and of a sound mind.* (2 Timothy 1:7 emphasis added)

*You must **not fear** them, for the Lord your God himself fights for you.* (Deuteronomy 3:22)

Praise God. No truck has dared to pull up to my home and steal from me. Whatever your concern, whatever your struggle, find God's promises regarding how to combat the enemy in that particular area. Begin to **meditate** on, memorize, believe, claim, and be obedient to God's specific word and just watch how he comes through for you. God is a promise keeper. You can count on him staying true to his word.

Psalm 119:165 is a reminder of the peace that comes from trusting in and **meditating** on God's word. "Great peace have those who love your law, and nothing causes them to stumble." If we love God's word which implies obedience to him, then not only can we have the peace of God, we shall not fail at whatever he gives us to do.

Ask yourself:

What will I do today to live according to God's word?

*Whose life can I uplift regarding the word of God that I have **meditated** upon today?*

*How can I be more pleasing to God because of his word that I have **meditated** upon today?*

Sincere reading, believing in, **meditating** on, and living out the truths of God's word has life transforming power.

Action Steps

Do you need a life transformation? Do you desire more out of this life? Do you want your life to have such meaning and significance that it makes you want to hop out of bed each morning and face the challenges that each new day brings without fear? God wants you to have this and has made a way for you to do it.

Once you have accepted Jesus as your Lord and Savior, you are under the divine protection of God and he will fight for you. He will lead and guide you as you **meditate** on his word and make it a part of your very being. Find a Bible today and begin to **meditate** on the promises of God. Claim these promises as your very own as if God were speaking to you directly. He desires to have a personal relationship with you as you go about living this life. He will never leave you or forsake you. He is a promise keeper.

Here are a few promises that you can **meditate** on and begin to claim as your own starting today:

> *How blessed is the one who does not follow the advice of the wicked, or stand in the pathway with sinners, or sit in the assembly of scoffers. Instead he finds pleasure in obeying the LORD's commands; he meditates on his commands day and night. He is like a tree planted by flowing streams; it yields its fruit at the proper time, and its leaves never fall off. He succeeds in everything he attempts."* (Psalm 1:1-3 NET)

> *And my God will supply your every need according to his glorious riches in Christ Jesus.* (Philippians 4:19 NET)

> *Come to me (Jesus), all you who labor and are heavy laden, and I will give you rest. Take my yoke upon you and learn from me, for I am gentle and lowly in heart, and you*

will find rest for your souls. For my yoke is easy and my burden is light. (Matthew 11:28-29)

But all who listen to me (Jesus) will live in peace, untroubled by fear of harm. (Proverbs 1:33 NLT)

If you openly declare that Jesus is Lord and believe in your heart that God raised him from the dead, you will be saved. (Romans 10:9 NLT)

Sea of Galilee at Capernaum, Israel. July 2014

Chapter 13
"E" Is for Energized

Do not burn out; keep yourselves fueled and aflame. Be alert servants of the master, cheerfully expectant. Do not quit in hard times; pray all the harder. Help needy Christians; be inventive in hospitality. (Romans 12:11-13 MSG)

> *Have you not known? Have you not heard? The everlasting God, the* Lord, *the creator of the ends of the earth, neither faints nor is weary. His understanding is unsearchable. He gives power to the weak, and to those who have no might he increases strength. Even the youths shall faint and be weary, and the young men shall utterly fall, but those who wait on the* Lord *shall* **renew their strength**; *they shall mount up with wings like eagles, they shall run and not be weary, they shall walk and not faint.* (Isaiah 40:28-31)

H ave you not known? Have you not heard? Where have you been hiding? What rock has your head been stuck under? Do not act like you do not know that there is a God of the universe.

> *For that which is known about God is evident to them and made plain in their inner consciousness, because God [himself] has shown it to them. For ever since the creation of the world his invisible nature and attributes, that is, his eternal power and divinity, have been made intelligible and clearly discernible in and through the*

things that have been made (his handiworks). So [men] are without excuse [altogether without any defense or justification] because when they knew and recognized him as God, they did not honor and glorify him as God or give him thanks. But instead they became futile and godless in their thinking [with vain imaginings, foolish reasoning, and stupid speculations] and their senseless minds were darkened. (Romans 1:19-21 AMP)

Our God "never faints or gets weary." He is tireless and he promises to **energize** us if we wait on him. His "understanding is unsearchable" so we can never fully comprehend how he does what he does. Isaiah 55:9 reminds us, "For *as* the heavens are higher than the earth, so are my ways higher than your ways and my thoughts than your thoughts."

No one can keep up with young children. They seem to run on energy that is constantly refueled. When our children were younger, even when they would come home from kindergarten with every manner of virus and cold possible, they would be running around even with rivers of mucous running from their noses. Meanwhile, we would be half dead from catching their disease, lying on the couch, praying they would run out of gas and fall asleep. I honestly did not think we would survive the first few years our boys were in school with all of the infectious diseases they would bring home to our house. Even their youthful energy cannot compare to the tirelessness of God. In fact even strong, courageous, young soldiers who are eager to fight in defense of their country could never stand up to the strength of God.

One of the keys to constantly renewing our strength is waiting on God. We do not like to wait, we like to go and do and take care of the problem so that we can be done with that task and move on to the next. We think that our progress gives us energy, but in God's system our energy comes from waiting on him. It has been said that an eagle can fly so high and powerfully that it can fly through and over torrential storms. When we quietly and patiently wait for the Holy Spirit to speak, and completely obey what he whispers, we will have this same capability and energy even in the midst of the worst storm we can imagine.

After we have done all he has asked of us, our job now consists of standing on his promises and waiting for him to fight for us. We serve a mighty God of action, and while we are waiting on him, he is energizing us as he is fighting on our behalf. Consider as further evidence to these truths, two of many scriptures I have written out on index cards to carry in my pocket and have buried in my heart.

The LORD is my rock and my fortress and my deliverer; the God of my strength, in whom I will trust; my shield and the horn of my salvation, my stronghold and my refuge; my savior, **you save me from violence***.* (2 Samuel 22:2-3 emphasis added)

The LORD will go forth like a warrior, he will arouse his zeal like a man of war. He will utter a shout, yes, he will raise a war cry. He will prevail against his enemies. (Isaiah 42:13 NASB)

It is the Lord going forth and not me. He alone is arousing his zeal. I should prayerfully consider maintaining a posture of praise and expectant hope, gaining more strength and energy as I rest and wait on the Lord to prevail as opposed to me expending my energy on worthless worry, needless anxiety, taxing bitterness, and sinful anger toward those who I perceive to be my enemies. Notice there is no battle to speak of. There is no back and forth exchange of bullets or rockets. There is no strategizing amongst the generals and commanders. There are no negotiations, phony peace accords or cease fires for humanitarian relief. There is only decisive victory for God. He will prevail.

God knows who my enemies are, what they are up to, and just how to defeat them. Psalm 18:47-48 reminds me that I can rest in and wait on the Lord to deliver me from my enemies, "He is the God who punishes my enemies for me, the one who puts people under my control. He saves me from my enemies. You, Lord, help me defeat those who attack me. You save me from cruel people" (ERV).

God will take care of his obedient children. He will do what needs to be done by whatever means he knows to be best. Our level of direct action may range from little to none or going all out at the battle front in the heat of the action. When and if he desires for us to act, we can be sure that he will energize us so that we can mount up with wings like eagles and are able to fly through and even over any war storms of life. I like the way Psalm 18:29 puts it, "For by you I can run against a troop, by my God I can leap over a wall." Now that is energized and worth shouting about.

After This…Stand and Smile

> *And the LORD restored the fortunes of Job when he had prayed for his friends; and the LORD gave job twice as much as he had before. Then there came to him all his brothers and sisters and all who had known him before,*

and they ate bread with him in his house; they showed him sympathy and comforted him for all the evil that the LORD had brought upon him; and each of them gave him a piece of money and a gold ring. The LORD blessed the latter days of Job more than his beginning; and he had fourteen thousand sheep, six thousand camels, a thousand yoke of oxen, and a thousand donkeys. He also had seven sons and three daughters. He named the first Jemimah, the second Keziah, and the third Keren-Happuch. In all the land there were no women so beautiful as Job's daughters; and their father gave them an inheritance along with their brothers. **After this** *Job lived one hundred and forty years, and saw his children, and his children's children, four generations. And Job died, old and full of day.* (Job 42:10-17 NRSV)

After this…after the storm, after the rain…after this.
After this…after the affliction, after the pain…after this.
After this…after the divorce, after the kids rebel…after this.
After this…after friends forsake you, after the church snubs you… after this.

After this…after the bankruptcy, after the business fails…after this.

After this… after you flunk out, after you are rejected…after this.

After this…after the bad doctors report, after the sickness…after this.

After this…after the suicide, after the homicide…after this.

After this… after the downside, after the bottom side…after this.

God is an "after this" God. Just like he was not finished with Job after all of the disasters he faced, he is not yet finished with you. You are not disqualified. Your story is not over. Because of Job's obedience, God had greater blessings for him after the storm was over, after he weathered the trial, and after he withstood all that the devil threw at him.

Just like God gave Job an "after this" experience, he wants to do the same for you and me. No matter what we have been through and no matter how painful, God wants you to experience his unspeakable joy that no one on this earth could possibly provide. A joy and peace that no euphoric substance could ever bring about is available from our loving God. A joy, peace, and provision that could only come as a result of a loving God sending his only Son, Jesus to die a horrendous death on a Roman crucifixion cross so that we might enjoy eternal salvation and a sweet fellowship with him. For nothing is impossible for our God. The sovereign God of this universe wants you and me to have "all-access" to his throne room and the power thereof so that we can overcome any adversity that comes our way.

Action Steps

How can we gain this access to almighty God?

How can we have God fight all of our battles?

How can we be energized even in the face of the most egregious attacks on our families, marriages, health, finances or any area of our lives?

The answer is really quite simple, accept Jesus as your Lord and obediently trust him to handle everything. Today is the day to stop fighting in your own strength which is never good enough for any lasting quality, and relinquish control of your life to the one and only, all-knowing, all-powerful, everywhere-all-the-time King Jesus who can never fail.

Right now, wherever you are, stop and say this:

Lord Jesus, I am tired. I cannot go on like this. I am exhausted. It seems like every time I take one step forward, a setback occurs and I take two steps back. My life is going nowhere fast. Lord Jesus, you said that those who put their trust in you will have renewed strength (be energized) and that you will fight their battles. I need that strength that only comes after inviting you to have total rule over my life's direction. Almighty God, in an act of faith, I believe that you personally love me so much that you sent your Son Jesus to shed his blood and die on a cross to pay the penalty for my sins. I know and freely admit that there are things that I have done that are wrong and I am sorry. I ask your forgiveness and right now, I am resolved to turn away from, and have nothing to do with anything that is not pleasing to you. Lord Jesus, you said that you are the way, the truth, and the life and that there is no other way to God, but through you alone. Therefore, Jesus, I claim you now as my Lord and Savior and renounce all other gods and all other ways to heavenly salvation and "paradise." I ask you to energize me, fill me with your hope, and give me a fresh new beginning. Just as I have asked you to forgive me, I choose to forgive those who have hurt and offended me. I trust you to deal with my offenders while I live a wonderfully peaceful life, free of any guilt, shame or bitterness. This is my prayer spoken by the authority of Jesus' name, Amen.

Playa Del Carmen, Mexico. July 2014

Conclusion
It Is P.R.O.O.F. T.I.M.E.

Know that because of your **praise** during the storm; because you chose to **remember** what your God had done for you in the past; because of your **obedience**; because you decided to **focus** on the victory already won by Jesus; because of your **trust** in the Master; because of your **intercession** for others in spite of your own pain; because of your specific **meditation** on God's word; and because you listened for and heeded the voice of the Holy Spirit, allowing the Almighty to **energize** you, **he has greater in store for you as well.** Whatever your particular "after this" experience is, know that God has now put before you a choice.

> *I call heaven and earth as witnesses today against you, that I have set before you life and death, blessing and cursing; therefore **choose life**, that both you and your descendants may live; that you may love the Lord your*

God, that you may obey his voice, and that you may cling to him, for he is your life and the length of your days; and that you may dwell in the land which the Lord swore to your fathers, to Abraham, Isaac, and Jacob, to give them. (Deuteronomy 30:19-20)

After this, choose life.

After this, choose blessings.

After this and from now on, stand, smile and choose **P.R.O.O.F. T.I.M.E.** (Praise-Remember-Obedience-Obedience-Focus-Trust-Inspire-Meditate-Energized) as your response to any adversity. In doing so you are choosing life and blessings everlasting.

Akko, Israel. July 2014

Welcome to God's Family

If you just said that prayer and sincerely meant it in your heart, then welcome to the family of God's redeemed. Your name is now written in heaven in the "Book of Life." All of the promises and blessings discussed in this book and the Bible are for you. If you have availed yourself of this greatest gift from God, then find a Jesus centered, Bible-believing and teaching church. Start reading the Bible which is really God speaking to you. Tell another Christ-follower that you have accepted Jesus as your Lord. Start speaking to God, sharing what is on your heart and then sit quietly to hear his sweet gentle whisper back to you. This is called prayer and it is a two way conversation. Watch and see how he will begin to reveal himself to you more and more as you grow closer to him in a specialized personal relationship that will be like no other.

I must also be truthful and tell you that if you have still not accepted God's free gift of salvation through believing in Jesus Christ, you are in severe danger. If you continue to reject Jesus as the only way to salvation and heaven, you are in severe danger. Severe danger of what you ask? Read God's word for yourself as written in Revelation 20:10-15.

> *Then the devil who had led them astray [deceiving and seducing them] was hurled into the fiery lake of burning brimstone, where the beast and false prophet were; and they will be tormented day and night forever and ever (through the ages of the ages). Then I saw a great white throne and the one who was seated upon it, from whose presence and from the sight of whose face earth and sky fled away, and no place was found for them. I [also]*

saw the dead, great and small; they stood before the throne, and books were opened. Then another book was opened, which is [the book] of life. And the dead were judged (sentenced) by what they had done [their whole way of feeling and acting, their aims and endeavors] in accordance with what was recorded in the books. And the sea delivered up the dead who were in it, death and hades (the state of death or disembodied existence) surrendered the dead in them, and all were tried and their cases determined by what they had done [according to their motives, aims, and works]. Then death and hades (the state of death or disembodied existence) were thrown into the lake of fire. This is the second death, the lake of fire. **And if anyone's [name] was not found recorded in the Book of Life, he was hurled into the lake of fire.** (AMP emphasis added)

Those who reject Jesus as Lord will not have their names written in the "Book of Life" and will suffer eternal separation from God and torment in hell, the lake of fire. This is the hard truth that I must share with you. Your decision to accept Jesus as your Lord and live out the wonderful promises of God recorded in the Bible will result in an eternity of joy in heaven. It is your decision that God has left completely up to you. When you come before God at the final judgment, you cannot claim that you did not know about Jesus. You have now been told. What will you do? Today is the day, now is the time, this is the place to accept God's free gift of salvation that can only come from accepting Jesus as Lord.

Island of Bora Bora, May 2014

Regardless of how bleak and desperate a seemingly insurmountable obstacle may appear, there is no need to become fearful, angry, discouraged or despondent. There is no need to get stuck in the *devil's ditch of "**d**'s"* where our ***d**isbelief,* our ***d**isobedience,* and our spiritual ***d**ysfunction* may cause us to choose to remain ***d**iscontented* and ***d**estitute*. In fact, this is really a time to give **praise** to our loving God because we can rest assured that if we patiently walk in obedience during the darkest hours of trial and tribulation, he will bring salvation. He will deliver his children from their bondage. He will provide and protect. This is the blessed assurance we have in God, our **hope**. Knowing that our God is sovereign, he alone is our help, and he has promised to help us in times of need. Not only should our final response to victory in the end be **praise,** but truly our first response to adversity should always be **praise** for we know how the story ends: *victory through Jesus.*

BORA BORA

Yes, I may be attacked by unjust people. Yes, the attack may seem so severe that I might be tempted to begin to think that God has rejected me. Yes, if not careful, I may walk with my head down, oppressed by the enemy. Yes, I may begin to question the seemingly unconquerable mountain that I may be climbing, but I am persuaded, I am blessedly assured that as I **wait** on the Lord in faithful obedience, he will intervene. For my God hears my cries for help. I have the benefit of knowing the end from the beginning, so I choose not to wait until the victory comes to fruition to begin to **praise** my God. Instead, I choose to make the painful hardship, the ram's horn sounding the alarm to begin shouting the **praises** of a victory that is sure to come.

Lord Jesus, I give you thanks. It is P.R.O.O.F. T.I.M.E.

There is hope.

Bora Bora

Turtle Sanctuary, Bora Bora

Bora Bora

Andre and Estomarys Mickel Honeymoon, early morning Tahiti heading to Bora Bora

Andre at the MLK Memorial, Wash. D.C. April, 2014

Andre and Estomarys Mickel Oct 2014 at the "100" Gala.

Epilogue
Brokenness Caused Me to Write This Book

I recall two rather odd phone calls I had received from my ex-wife in which she said that she never felt like she had a chance to be a mother to the boys, and that she wanted to keep the boys with her at all times. We had talked about a week before that and she had asked me if she could keep the boys with her. She said if I would agree then I would not have to pay her any money, and that she felt that if she did not try to help our sons now, that she would regret it the rest of her life. After praying and talking with my family counselor, advisors, close friends and family, I was certain that it would not be a good idea for her to keep the boys exclusively.

First of all, just a few weeks before that time, she was frantic on the phone saying that the boys always manipulated her and she was uncertain how to handle them. She had said that one of our sons in particular, never told her the truth, was putting horrendous things out on the internet that were dangerous to her well-being as she lived alone usually. Her new husband only came into town on selected weekends. She additionally commented that this same child needed psychological care and they both needed to be working this summer. She did not know what to do with them, but she definitely did not want them doing landscaping (which they enjoyed doing the previous summer) with their cousin whom she used to pay to take care of them at her house. Now however, she was no longer speaking to him.

Ironically, this cousin was perhaps an important reason why the court-ordered psychologist recommended she be granted joint custody with me. He was fired by my ex-wife soon after the divorce leaving no one to care for the boys, at which time they began to get into some trouble at her home when they were with her on her weeks. Apparently she was upset that the cousin did a background check on her present husband and claimed to have found out that he had criminal allegations involving prostitution and other crimes. The cousin and others in her family did not feel that this man should be trusted around the boys.

Anyway, at her request, I got them both a summer internship job at the church, which before confirming acceptance, I got her approval. Having just seen his psychologist, it was suggested that one of our sons get a psychiatric evaluation to rule out any disorders. I immediately took the opportunity to give my ex-wife the name of an adolescent psychologist, to have her call and talk to the doctor to see if she were acceptable to her. I did this because in the six years that I had been taking my children to see a child psychologist to help deal with the emotional distress of family separation and strife, my ex-wife had come with us only three times, and that was only because her psychiatrist told her that she needed to be a part of any therapy the children were undergoing, and that as their mother, she should want to know what was going on with her children.

Her excuse for not coming was that she felt that nothing was wrong with the children, she did not believe in psychological therapy, the psychologist was just trying to help me take her children away from her, and that she never agreed to them going to the psychologist. All of this in spite of the school they were attending even strongly suggesting we get them to a psychologist from the beginning some six years ago. When the school requested that we get them to a psychologist, I (and many family and friends) knowing that some intervention was and had been needed had already gotten a recommendation from the chief of staff of one of the local major hospitals and had an appointment scheduled already for the next week. The school was very pleased, and my ex-wife was very relieved and grateful that I was already in compliance

IT'S PROOF TIME...

with the school's request. Nevertheless, she never went to our weekly/bi-weekly appointments with the children's psychologist ever in the first three years and later again only three times at the insistence of her own psychiatrist.

So now she is asking to keep the kids with her instead of our week at a time exchange, and she still had not called the psychiatrist to schedule an appointment, or to even see if the doctor was acceptable to her. The only reason that I did not call and schedule the appointment myself was because in order for any doctor's therapy to be helpful, both parents would have to completely buy in and participate. She had certainly appeared to continuously undermine the work of the present psychologist, so I needed her to agree to the doctor chosen and thereby have no excuses not to participate in therapy. I was ready and willing to go to any appointments that she could make at her own convenience. She had already just a few weeks before admitted that she could not control them and that they take advantage of her and manipulate her to get whatever they want.

I must confess that now as she was asking me if I would allow her to keep our sons because she said that she has never had a chance to be a mother, I was thinking to myself, "Just where have you been and just what have you been doing for the past fifteen years?"

Taking the advice of my family therapist of over three years, I very politely said, "I just do not believe that to be a good idea."

I also said that I hoped that she had not said anything to the boys about this because there is a court order in place for a good reason. Furthermore, she should not be having any negative conversations with them regarding them having a relationship with me in any way. I reminded her that there are many people who love and care for the boys including their grandma, numerous close family, friends, pastors, professionals and certainly me, their father.

This infuriated her even more and now the truth came out of her mouth, "Since you choose to be unreasonable and not let me keep the boys even though I am not asking you to pay any money, I need to let you know that the boys and I have already talked about all of this and we have decided that they are going to stay with me."

Not wanting to get drawn into a combative and really unnecessary argument, I told her that I was not even going to address that because there was already a court order in place that I would appreciate her following.

Apparently just before July 5th one of the boys had told her that he did not want to work and that they could not believe that she had agreed with me regarding them working this summer church job. She now denied agreeing with me for them to work at the church. The July 5th phone call ended with her saying she was going to keep the boys and that there was nothing I or anyone else could do about it. I again reminded her of the court order that was still in place.

Interestingly, she called me back a little while later acting very oddly quiet and subdued, nothing like the loud screaming person I talked to just an hour ago. She began to speak as if we had never had that confrontation earlier. She then asked if I was off of work that day and at home which I told her I was.

She then said, "So you are really not going to let me keep the boys?"

I replied again, "I do not believe that to be a good idea, so sorry, no."

So we now fast forward to later that same day when I went to pick up the children from church, and was informed they were picked up by their mother around noon. I called my ex-wife on the phone, she sarcastically reminded me that she told me that she was taking the boys, and that there was nothing I could do about it. I again reminded her that this was a violation of the court order and to please drop them off at my home. She said she would not do so and then hung up.

Neither I, their grandma, their psychologist, or many close family and friends saw them again from the time I last dropped them off for work at the church June 28, 2013 until December. They have never seen their psychologist again as my ex-wife still refuses to take them. One of my sons ended up in the emergency room with severe chest pains, and my ex-wife never bothered to even inform me.

In spite of a standing court order in Cuyahoga County Domestic Relations Court, in Cleveland, Ohio, for me to have parenting time with my children on a weekly basis as the residential parent for school and other purposes, I feel as if my rights have been completely, painfully, and quite frankly, abusively denied. This drama is still unfolding, but if it had not been for this painful adversarial trial, I probably would not have started to write this book.

I do not know how this will end, but I do know God is still reigning and ruling and worthy of my praise. Therefore, I have decided that instead of allowing hurt, pain, abandonment, and the desire to retaliate to trap me in a lost sea of bitterness, I will instead fill my mouth, heart, and mind with continual praise as I pray for God's perfect peace, provision, patience, presence, and will all in his perfect timing.

Appendix 1
Suggested Reading

May I suggest a wonderful daily devotional book series written by Sue Piper and Sandy Petty, *God Whispers,* available directly from the authors @ sandpiper1122@gmail.com or from most major book publishers. Each of these devotional books have short but action-packed and thought provoking daily readings that will encourage you as you face the challenges of living to your fullest every day. Each daily reading will only take you less than five minutes to read, but I am excited to tell you, may provide hours of feasting and meditating on the word of the Lord. This devotional book series has quickly become one of my favorite and I am pleased to be able to personally recommend it to you.

One of the authors, Sue Piper was a patient of mine who came in one day and just happened to ask if I would be willing to put her devotional books in my office reception room for patients to read while waiting to be seen. As she sat in my chair (to have a root canal performed.), I took the books into my office and opened one of them to the daily reading for that particular date. I was amazed at how the words quickly grabbed me and spoke directly to my heart, even to what was happening that very day. I immediately told her that unfortunately, I could not put those books in my reception room because I would be keeping these books for myself. Before you are too harsh on me, I actually ordered forty more of their books, so that I could not only put some in my reception room, I immediately began to give them out as gifts. Everyone who has read them has said that they can feel the presence of God actually speaking directly to their hearts. I know this to be true for me as well.

Appendix 2
Application of Matthew 17:14-20

What are some lessons for Christ-followers that can be gleaned from Matthew 17:14-20? First, just as the man came and knelt before Jesus and asked for mercy, we must always begin everything we do, with coming before our Lord Jesus in worship and praise. We must acknowledge that he alone is Lord, and we have no other place to go. No one else can help, nor do we even desire to align ourselves with anyone but the sovereign God of the universe. Matthew reminds us in 6:33 to "strive first for the kingdom of God and his righteousness…" (NRSV).

Second, Jesus cares about whatever is troubling us. Just as the father was crying out on behalf of his epileptic and demon-possessed son, who would often fall into the fire and water, we too can cry out to our Lord, because he hears and he cares. **Every affliction, every pain, every sorrow, every fall (and we will all fall into a trial by**

fire sooner or later), he cares. Matthew ends his gospel with Jesus commissioning the disciples to "go therefore and make disciples of all nations… and remember, I am with you always…" If the mission of the church is not to make disciples, then simply put, we are not being obedient to the Savior, who willingly died to provide a means for our salvation, and for whom discipleship was so important.

This third point, is so important, because while Jesus asked in Matthew 17:17, how much longer he must be with them (implying that he would soon be gone from their presence), he leaves them this encouraging reminder now at the end of the gospel before his ascension, "…remember, I am with you always." Because Jesus is "always" with us, Christ-followers should be encouraged and thus empowered to fulfill the commission. He would never ask us to do anything that he has not equipped us to do. We should therefore, walk in the authority of our risen king.

Fourth, there is power in the word of Jesus and there is power in Jesus, the living word. Note that the instant Jesus rebuked the demon in Matthew 17:18, "the boy was instantly cured." When we stand on the word of God, we are standing on the guaranteed promises of God, ratified by the shed blood of Jesus in his death, and confirmed by the glory of his resurrection.

Fifth, when in doubt, just ask the Lord. The disciples asked Jesus why they could not cast out the demon. Jesus freely and clearly answered their question. When we lack wisdom, our omniscient God in James 1:5 tells us to ask him. Simple as that, just ask the question. Confessing that we do not have the answer, but we are seeking the truth of God. We are seeking the perfect will of God in the perfect timing of God. As we are seeking to be pleasing to God, he provides his perfect peace and his perfect provision. God honors such requests for his truth.

Finally, and key to the passage of Matthew 17:14-20, we must have faith. Hebrews 11:6 magnifies the importance that God puts on faith, "and without faith, it is **impossible** to please [God]..." (NRSV) note the word "impossible." Faith is an essential mandatory prerequisite for relationship with God that no one can circumvent.

Note God's repetition of man pursuing other things in addition to faith throughout his word. For instance, 1 Timothy 6:11, "But you, o man of God, flee these things and pursue righteousness, godliness, faith, love, patience, gentleness." Or consider 2 Timothy 2:22, "Flee also youthful lusts; but pursue righteousness, faith, love, peace with those who call on the Lord out of a pure heart."

Again, while faith is absolutely essential to our relationship with Christ Jesus, it is the starting point. Nevertheless, the word of God is clear in Hebrews 11:

By faith, we understand that the worlds were framed by the word of God (v3).

By faith, Abel offered God an excellent sacrifice (v4).

By faith, Enoch pleased God and did not see death (v5).

By faith, Noah built an ark to save his family (v7).

By faith, Abraham obeyed God and left not knowing where he was going (v8).

By faith, Sarah bore a child in her old age (v11).

By faith, Abraham offered Isaac as a sacrifice (v17).

By faith, Joseph instructed his bones be taken from Egypt when freed (v22).

By faith, Moses' parents were not afraid and hid him when he was born (v23).

By faith, Moses chose to suffer with the people of God and forsook Egypt (v25-27).

By faith, Moses kept the Passover and sprinkling of blood to save the firstborn (v28).

By faith, Israel walked on dry ground through the red sea (v29).

By faith, the walls of Jericho fell down after seven days (v30).

By faith, a harlot named Rahab was spared and became a part of the family of Jesus (v31).

By faith, David subdued kingdoms (v33).

By faith, Daniel stopped the mouth of lions (v33).

By faith, Shadrach, Meshach and Abednego quenched the violence of fire (v34).

By faith, Gideon became valiant in battle (v34).

By faith, the widow of Zarephath's dead son was raised to life by Elijah (v35/1 Kings 17:22).

By faith, the Shulammite's dead son was raised to life by Elisha (v35/2 Kings 4:32-35).

By faith, many others obtained a good testimony, but did not receive the promise.

APPENDIX 3
THERE IS HOPE

Let us consider the term **hope** as found in Psalm 43:5, "Why are you cast down, O my soul, and why are you disquieted within me? **Hope** in God; for I shall again praise him, my help and my God." The Hebrew word for **hope** in Psalm 43:5 is הוֹחִילִי *(hō·w·ḥî·lî)*. The root word is יָחַל (yachal) which carries the idea of waiting for, cause to wait, or tarrying for.[53] Lamp notes that while our current day use of the word **hope** enjoins the uncertain with a wishful outcome, biblical **hope** is much more complex and is associated with a faith founded on God and his promises.[54] There are other Hebrew words which have varying meanings of **hope/wait**. For instance תִּקְוָה *(tiqvah)* is a noun which implies looking forward to a positive outcome as in Psalm 9:18, "For the needy shall not always be forgotten, nor the **hope** of the poor perish forever." קָוָה *(qavah)* is used as a verb and in Psalm 56:5 means

---

[53] Francis Brown, S.R. Driver, and Charles A. Briggs, *A Hebrew and English Lexicon of the Old Testament* (Oxford: Clarendon, 1978).

[54] Jeffrey Lamp, "Hope" in *Eerdmans Dictionary of the Bible* (Grand Rapids: Eerdmans Publishing Company: Grand Rapids, 2000), 605.

to **wait for** "...as they have **waited** to take my life." In Jeremiah 14:8, there is the use of the Hebrew word מִקְוֵה *(miqveh)* used as a proper noun referring to **God, their hope:** "O **hope of Israel**, its savior in times of distress..."[55]

Illumination from Parallel Usages of the Word "Hope"

The use of the word **hope** with יָחַל*(yachal)* as the Hebrew root is not only seen in the selected passage (Psalm 43:5), but can also be found in the preceding Psalm 42 in verses 5 and 11, where the entire verses are directly repeated. The New English translation for these same three verses renders the word **wait in place of hope**: "Why are you depressed, O my soul? Why are you upset? **Wait** for God. For I will again give thanks to my God for his saving intervention." This repetition is obviously intentional in drawing on the fact that the only **hope** one really ever has of overcoming any adversity with complete victory, is to **wait** for the solution supplied by God.

In Psalm 119:43, 49, 74, 81, 114, and 147 speaking of God's law or word, it is not surprising to see **hope** in not only God, but in his word. For we know that God cannot lie and that unlike man, he is a promise-keeper. Note Psalm 119:81, "My soul languishes for your

---

[55] BDB, *Hebrew and English Lexicon*

salvation; I **hope** in your word." God promises salvation to those who trust in him and thus his word. Or consider Psalm 119:114, "You are my hiding place and my shield; I **hope** in your word." God promises protection to those who obey his word.

BIBLIOGRAPHY

Aquinas, Thomas. *"Summa Theologiae,"* in *the Christian Theology Reader,* ed. Allister E. McGrath. West Sussex: Wiley-Blackwell publishing, 2011.

Barclay, W. *Flesh and Spirit: An Examination of Galatians 5:19-23.* London: SCM, 1962.

Barton, S. C. "faith" in *Dictionary of Jesus and the Gospels.* Ed., Andrew T. Le Peu. Downers Grove: Intervarsity Press, 1992.

Bauer, David R. *The structure of Matthew's Gospel: A study in literary design.* Journal for the study of the New Testament supplement series, 31. Sheffield: Almond Press, 1988.

Beale, G. K. "The Old Testament background of Paul's reference to 'the Fruit of the Spirit' in Galatians 5:22." *Bulletin for biblical research* 15 (2005): 1-38.

Brand, Chad Owen, Charles W. Draper and Archie W. England, ed. *Holman Illustrated Bible Dictionary.* Nashville: Holman Bible publishers, 2003.

Brown, Francis, S.R. Driver and Charles A. Briggs. *A Hebrew and English Lexicon of the Old Testament.* Oxford: Clarendon, 1978.

Davies, W. D. and D. C. Allison. *Matthew 8-18,* Vol. 3 International Critical Commentary, edited by J. A. Emerton, C. E. B. Cranfield and G. N. Stanton. New York: T&T Clark ltd, 1991.

DeSilva, David A. *An Introduction to the New Testament.* Downers Grove: Intervarsity Press, 2004.

Dunn, D. G., and John W. Rogerson, ed. *Eerdmans Commentary on the Bible.* Grand Rapids, Michigan: Eerdmans, 2003

France, R. T. *The Gospel of Matthew,* the New International Commentary on the New Testament. Grand Rapids, Michigan: William B. Eerdmans publishing company, 2007.

Freedman, David Noel, ed. *Eerdmans Dictionary of the Bible.* Grand Rapids, Michigan: Eerdmans, 2000.

Gaventa, Beverly Roberts and David Petersen, ed. *The New Interpreter's Bible one Volume Commentary.* Nashville, TN: Abingdon Press, 2010.

Geddert, T. J. "peace," in *Dictionary of Jesus and the Gospels.* Ed., Andrew T. Le Peu. Downers Grove: Intervarsity, 1992.

Grenz, Stanley, David Guretzki and Cherith Fee Nordling. *Pocket Dictionary of Theological Terms*. Downers Grove, Illinois: Intervarsity Press, 1990.

Gundry, Robert H. *Matthew:* A *Commentary on his Literary and Theological Art.* Grand rapids, Michigan: William B. Eerdmans Publishing Company, 1982.

Hagner, Donald A. *Matthew 14-28,* vol. 33b Word Biblical Commentary, edited by David A. Hubbard, Glenn W. Barker and Bruce Metzger. Nashville: Thomas Nelson, 1995.

Jinkins, Michael. *Invitation to Theology*. Downers Grove, Illinois: Intervarsity Press, 2001.

Kingsbury, J.D. "The Structure of Matthew's Gospel and his Concept of Salvation-history." *The Catholic Biblical Quarterly* 35 (1973): 451-474.

Kotansky, R. "Demonology," in *Dictionary of New Testament Background,* edited by Craig A. Evans and Stanley E. Porter, 269-273, Downers Grove: Intervarsity Press, 2000.

Lamp, Jeffrey. "hope" in *Eerdmans Dictionary of the Bible*. Grand Rapids, Michigan: William B. Eerdmans Publishing Company, 2000.

Longenecker, Richard N. *Galatians: Word Biblical Commentary.* Nashville: Thomas Nelson, 1990.

Luz, Ulrich. *The theology of the gospel of Matthew,* New Testament theology, translated by J. Bradford Robinson. Edited by James D. G. Dunn. New York: Cambridge University Press, 1995.

McGrath, Alister E., ed. *The Christian Theology Reader.* West Sussex: Wiley-Blackwell Publishing, 2011.

Painter, John. "The Fruit of the Spirit Is Love: Galatians 5:22-23, an exegetical note." *Journal of Theology for Southern Africa.* (1973): 57-59.

Patte, Daniel. *The gospel according to Matthew: a structural commentary on Matthew's faith.* Philadelphia: Fortress Press, 1987.

Sakenfeld, Katharine Doob, ed. *The New Interpreter's Dictionary of the Bible, vol.2.* Nashville, Tn.: Abingdon Press, 2007

Senior, Donald. *Matthew,* Abingdon New Testament commentaries, edited by Victor Paul Furnish. Nashville: Abingdon Press, 1998.

_____.*The Gospel of Matthew, interpreting biblical texts,* edited by Gene M. Tucker and Charles B. Cousar. Nashville: Abingdon Press, 1997.

Twelftree, G. H. "demon, devil, Satan," in *Dictionary of Jesus and the Gospels*, edited by   Andrew T. Le Peu, 163-172. Downers Grove: Intervarsity, 1992.

Wire, Antoinette C. "Gender Roles in a Scribal Community," in *Social History of the Matthean Community: Cross-disciplinary Approaches*, edited by David L. Balch, 87-121. Minneapolis: Fortress Press, 1991.

Twelftree, G. H. "demon, devil, Satan," in *Dictionary of Jesus and the Gospels*, edited by Andrew T. Le Peu, 163-172. Downers Grove: Intervarsity, 1992.

Wire, Antoinette C. "Gender Roles in a Scribal Community," in *Social History of the Matthean Community: Cross-disciplinary Approaches*, edited by David L. Balch, 87-121. Minneapolis: Fortress Press, 1991.

CPSIA information can be obtained at www.ICGtesting.com
Printed in the USA
BVOW11s0249200215

388382BV00003B/5/P